Reconcilable rights

analysing the tension between victims and defendants

rethinking
CRIME & PUNISHMENT

This project has been funded by *Rethinking Crime and Punishment* – a strategic initiative of the Esmée Fairbairn Foundation designed to raise the level of public debate about the use of prison and alternative forms of punishment in the UK.

The Legal Action Group is a national, independent charity that campaigns for equal access to justice for all members of society. Legal Action Group:
- provides support to the practice of lawyers and advisers
- inspires developments in that practice
- campaigns for improvements in the law and the administration of justice
- stimulates debate on how services should be delivered.

Reconcilable rights?

analysing the tension between victims and defendants

edited by Ed Cape

Legal Action Group
2004

Published in Great Britain 2004
by LAG Education and Service Trust Limited
242 Pentonville Road, London N1 9UN
www.lag.org.uk

British Library Cataloguing in Publication Data
a CIP catalogue record for this book is available from the British Library.

ISBN 1 903307 31 7

Typeset by Regent Typesetting, London.
Printed in Great Britain by Hobbs the Printers, Totton, Hampshire.

Acknowledgements

Legal Action Group gratefully acknowledges Rethinking Crime and Punishment (a strategic initiative of the Esmée Fairbairn Foundation) for funding this book and for supporting the series of seminars on which it is based. Thanks are also due to Clifford Chance and Bindman & Partners for hosting the seminar series in 2003.

Contents

Contributors

Ed Cape is Professor of Criminal Law and Practice at the University of the West of England, Bristol. Formerly a partner in a legal aid solicitors' practice, he has been involved with the Legal Action Group (as management committee member and associate) for many years, and was a member of the Law Society's Criminal Law Committee from 1994 to 2003. He wrote the Committee's guidance for criminal defence lawyers, *Police Station Advice: Advising on Silence* (October 2003). His research interests include criminal evidence and procedure, the criminal defence profession and access to justice. Jointly with Andrew Sanders, Carolyn Hoyle and Rod Morgan he was involved in the evaluation of the victim statement pilots, and he is currently a member of the team evaluating the Public Defender Service. His publications include *Defending Suspects at Police Stations* (4th ed, LAG, 2003), and he writes regularly for a number of journals including *Criminal Law Review* and *Legal Action*.

Paul Clark is the member of parliament for Gillingham in Kent, elected in 1997, and Assistant Government Whip since June 2003. He served as Parliamentary Private Secretary to Lord Falconer, in his capacity as Secretary of State for Constitutional Affairs and in his previous capacity as Minister of State for Housing at DTLR. Paul is also a member of the Labour Party Backbench Committee on Home Affairs. Prior to this Paul worked in various positions within the Amalgamated Engineering Union (now Amicus) and then was centre manager for the TUC National Education Centre from 1986 to 1997.

Sandra Walklate is Professor of Sociology at Manchester Metropolitan University. She has worked extensively with police officers and victim support workers both as a trainer and as a volunteer throughout her academic career. Sandra's research interests have focused latterly on crime and the fear of crime with a particular focus on how people construct their sense of security. She is author of various publications on criminology and victimology, including *Gender, Crime and Criminal Justice* (2001).

J. R. Spencer QC has been a Professor of Law at the University of Cambridge since 1995. From 1990 onwards he has also spent a number of periods at French universities as a visiting professor. His interests include criminal evidence and comparative criminal procedure. He was part of the international team of criminal lawyers that produced the EU *Corpus Juris* project. In England, he was a consultant to Lord Justice Auld's Review of the Criminal Courts (which reported in October 2001). His publications include the 8th edition of *Jackson's Machinery of Justice* (1989), (with Rhona Flin), *The Evidence of Children, the Law and the Psychology* (2nd ed, 1993), *La procédure pénale anglaise* (Que sais-je? series) (1998), and (with Mireille Delmas-Marty) *European Criminal Procedures* (2002).

Jane Hickman was admitted as a solicitor in 1977, and worked in Law Centres and at a trade union before joining Fisher Meredith in 1980, becoming a partner in 1983 and head of criminal department in 1985. In 1991 she set up Hickman and Rose, specialising in crime and human rights, now one of London's largest criminal firms, where she is currently managing partner. Jane is secretary to the Criminal Appeal Lawyers Association and a past Committee member of South London Law Society, London Legal Aid Area Committee and the Legal Action Group. She was a consultant to Lord Justice Auld's Review of the Criminal Courts 2000–01. Jane Hickman writes and lectures on the quality and delivery of publicly funded legal services.

John Jackson was called to the Bar of Northern Ireland in 1977 and to the English Bar in 1985. He was appointed lecturer in Law at Queen's University Belfast in 1980 and became Reader in Law in 1990 and Professor of Public Law in 1995. He has taught in a number of other law schools and was a visiting professor at Hastings College of the Law, University of California in 2000. From 1998–2000 he was an independent assessor on the Northern Ireland Criminal Justice Review which was established to review the Northern Ireland criminal justice system. He was appointed a research panellist on the Arts and Humanities Research Board in September 2001.

Edna Erez is Professor of Justice Studies at Kent State University. Her research areas include comparative justice, sociology of law, victims and immigrants in the justice system, and violence against women, on which she has published extensively in journals such as *Criminology, Justice Quarterly, Crime & Delinquency, Criminal Law Review*. She has served on the editorial boards of several major professional journals in criminology, victimology and criminal justice. Edna Erez has been Visiting Professor at Warsaw University, University of Melbourne and Haifa University and resident scholar at the Australian Institute of Criminology and the Max Planck Institute for Comparative Criminal Law in Freiburg, Germany. She has served on review panels for the US National Institute of Justice and served as a consultant on victim participation in justice to the governments of the United States, Australia, Canada and Israel.

Andrew Sanders is Allen & Overy Professor of Criminal Law and Criminology at the University of Manchester. His research interests include the role of victims in the criminal justice process and the special measures available in the pre-trial and trial process to help vulnerable and intimidated witnesses to testify. He is currently writing a book on victim participation in criminal justice. Andrew (with Ed Cape, Carolyn Hoyle and Rod Morgan) was involved in evaluating the VIS pilot projects, now called 'Personal Statements'. His publications include *The Case for the Prosecution* (1991) and *Criminal Justice* (2nd ed, 2000). He was, until recently, a member of the Parole Board for England & Wales. He is currently a Life Sentence Review Commissioner for Northern Ireland and a member of the Crown Prosecution Service Inspectorate Advisory Board.

Barbara Hudson is Professor of Law at the University of Central Lancashire. Her main research interests are in race and criminal justice, feminist jurisprudence, desert theory, restorative justice, comparative criminology and penology. She is an advisory board member of the Centre for Penal Theory and Penal Ethics, and on the editorial board of the *British Journal of Criminology* and *Punishment and Society*. Barbara Hudson is author of *Justice through Punishment* (1987); *Penal Policy and Social Justice* (1993); *Understanding Justice* (2nd ed, 2003) and *Justice in the Risk Society* (2003).

Francesca Klug is a professorial research fellow at the London School of Economics' Centre for the Study of Human Rights and director of the new Human Rights Futures Project. Francesca was formerly a senior research fellow at King's College London law school. Acknowledged as one of the driving forces behind the UK's Human Rights Act, she worked with politicians and civil servants to develop a model for incorporating the European Convention on Human Rights into UK law. For this she was awarded an OBE for services to human rights in the 2002 New Year's honours list and was joint winner of *The Times*/JUSTICE 1998 Human Rights awards. She is author of *Values for a Godless Age, the story of the UK's new bill of rights* (2000) and has written widely on human rights.

CHAPTER 1

Overview:
Is reconciliation possible?

By Ed Cape

Professor of Criminal Law and Practice, University of the West of England, Bristol

In April 2002 the Legal Action Group (LAG) held a seminar entitled *Defendants vs victims – a zero sum game?* The purpose was to explore the tensions between the interests of victims and those of defendants in the criminal process. LAG, an organisation committed to promoting access to justice, was concerned about the way in which successive governments during the 1990s and first years of the twenty-first century were presenting the relationship between victims' and defendants' rights as a central feature of criminal justice policy. In particular, it was disturbed by the growing polarisation of the rights and interests of victims and of those accused of crime in both government rhetoric and in popular discourse. LAG wanted to contribute to an understanding of why this was happening, whether the respective interests truly are irreconcilable, and how the debate might be steered on to a more rational, evidence-based, course.

That seminar was, in part, prompted by the white paper *Criminal Justice: the way ahead*[1] in which the government presented the relationship between the rights of victims and those of defendants as constituting a 'balance' whereby the rights of one party can only be achieved at the expense of the other.[2] This characterisation was not new, but it was becoming established as an incontrovertible 'truth'. In his *Review of the Criminal Courts* Lord Justice Auld suggested that a balance had to be struck 'between the community's interest in

---

1 Cm 5074.
2 The title of the seminar owed much to David Garland's analysis. See D. Garland, *The Culture of Control*, (Oxford University Press, 2001) esp pp142–145.   1

providing an efficient and economic system for administering justice
... and the manner of fair trial that it provides for offences of different
seriousness'.[3] It had to be remembered, he said, that criminal
processes 'are not just there to protect defendants':[4] until recently the
focus had been on the criminal or alleged criminal, 'leaving the vic
tim, or alleged victim, with only a walk-on part'.[5] Others were even
more forthright. Sir David Phillips, then president of the Association
of Chief Police Officers, felt able to state categorically that 'it is already
acknowledged in this country that victims' rights appear to come
second to the defendant's in court'.[6]

The government went a stage further in its next criminal justice
white paper, *Justice for All*, published in July 2002 in advance of the
criminal justice bill which was introduced into Parliament in November of the same year.[7] In a joint foreword by the Home Secretary, the
then Lord Chancellor and the Attorney-General, the government's
aim was described as being to 'rebalance the system in favour of
victims, witnesses and communities'. This phrase came to be used
frequently as the criminal justice bill made its controversial way
through the parliamentary process, re-appearing in the Home Office
press release issued on Royal Assent. The Prime Minister, Tony Blair,
in a major interview for *The Observer* timed to coincide with the
announcement of the bill in the 2002 Queen's Speech, presented the
case in stark 'zero-sum' terms: 'Justice [is] weighted towards the criminal and [is] in need of rebalancing towards the victim'.[8]

Despite this clearly expressed rationale for the legislation, the
criminal justice bill, which eventually received Royal Assent in
November 2003,[9] contained no explicit new rights for victims of
crime, a point made by many of the speakers and participants in the
seminar series which resulted in this book.[10] The government argued,

---

3   The Stationery Office, October 2001, p13.
4   ibid, p11.
5   ibid, p496.
6   Quoted in an ACPO press release dated 10 January 2002.
7   Cm 5563.
8   *The Observer*, 10 November 2002, p26.
9   The bill was significantly amended, especially in the House of Lords. For
    accounts of its passage see M. Zander, 'The Criminal Justice Bill gets Royal
    Assent' (2003) *New Law Journal*, 28 November, and E. Cape, 'Criminal Justice
    Act 2003 – no debate?' (2004) *Legal Action*, January p8.
10 Similar views were expressed at a Cambridge Crime Policy Conferences held in
    November 2002. See M. Tonry, *Confronting Crime: crime control policy under New
    Labour*, (Willan, 2003), esp p235.

however, that by making changes that would ensure that more criminals are caught and successfully prosecuted, victims would 'get a better deal' and communities would be 'properly protected through appropriate punishment for offenders that also seeks to rehabilitate and reduce the chances of further offending'. At the same time, the central principles of the criminal justice system, 'that a person is innocent until proven guilty and that jury trial is and should be the norm' would be preserved.[11] The Home Secretary also maintained that measures in the bill had been widely consulted upon and were designed to 'take forward' the recommendations of both the Law Commission and the independent reviews of Sir Robin Auld and John Halliday.[12]

It was in this context that LAG planned a series of seminars with the title *Reconciling rights in criminal justice*, to be held in the summer of 2003. The purpose was to explore the impact of the government's pursuit of a new 'balance' between victims' and defendants' rights, and the implications for the operation of criminal justice processes, and for outcomes within the criminal justice system. Being a non-aligned group, concerned with access to justice by all rather than having a partisan interest on behalf of victims or those suspected or accused of crime, LAG's aim was to promote understanding of the issues involved and, if necessary, some degree of reconciliation between various interest groups. As will be seen, such reconciliation hardly appeared necessary. During the course of the seminars it became apparent that the greatest gulf is that between the government and the various stakeholders. Although not exclusively so, most speakers and most participants appeared to agree that, to a large extent, the terms 'victim' and 'victimhood' have taken on a totemic meaning which is used by government with little apparent connection to the real needs of real victims.

In the event, four seminars were held on four separate, but interconnected themes: unravelling the political context; analysing recent

---

11 See Home Office press release 317/2002, issued on 21 November 2002. Jury trial is not, of course, 'the norm'. The vast majority of trials are conducted in magistrates' courts.

12 See, in particular, the three Law Commission reports *Evidence in Criminal Proceedings: Hearsay and Related Topics*, No 245 (TSO, London, 1997), *Double Jeopardy and Prosecution Appeals*, No 267, CM 5048 (TSO, London, 2000), and *Evidence of Bad Character in Criminal Proceedings*, No 273, CM 5257 (TSO, London, 2001); *Making Punishments Work*, Home Office, London, 2001 (The Halliday Report); *Review of the Criminal Courts of England and Wales* (October 2001) (The Auld Review). The Home Secretary's assertions are open to considerable doubt. See E. Cape, above, n9.

changes; involving victims in sentencing; and what rights should victims have? The first seminar was designed to examine the political context surrounding the policies concerning victims and defendants, and to give the government the opportunity to explain why it appears to believe that victims' and defendants' rights are mutually incompatible. Two specific questions were posed: what is the history of the tension between victims' and defendants' rights? And have political and policy developments in the criminal justice system contributed to the perceived conflict between these rights?

The second seminar, 'Analysing recent changes', examined the impact of recent changes to law and practice affecting victims and defendants, and pre-figured the likely impact of provisions of the criminal justice bill. Again, two specific questions were asked: to what extent are victims' interests actually served by the 'pro victim' changes introduced in recent years – or have false expectations been created? And what effect have these changes had on the defendant's right to fair trial? The third seminar, 'Involving victims in sentencing', provided an opportunity for two leading protagonists in the debate about victim impact statements to go 'head to head'. They were asked to consider a number of questions including whether there is justification for victims to have a role in the sentencing process, and whether restorative justice processes can 'square the circle' by offering advantages to both victims and defendants. The final seminar, entitled 'What rights should victims have?', gave speakers and delegates the opportunity to consider the principles that should inform policies and decisions concerning victims and defendants and, in the light of the previous seminars, to consider whether a consensus could be achieved on appropriate rights for victims within an adversarial system of criminal justice.

The speakers at the seminars, the authors of the papers in this volume, were drawn from a variety of backgrounds representing different perspectives. In order to promote a wide-ranging analysis and discussion of the issues, it was decided not to invite speakers from groups with well-established policies or positions on victims' or defendants' rights. The majority of the speakers were academics well known for their research and analysis relating to the issues. In addition, a number of legal practitioners were invited to speak and Lord Falconer (then a Home Office minister) was invited to explain the government's approach to its criminal justice policy in general, and its policies concerning victims and defendants in particular. In the event, Lord Falconer was prevented at the last minute by parliamentary business from appearing, and his place was taken by his parliamentary private secretary, Paul Clark MP.

One of the unfortunate features of the current political process is that there are too few opportunities for full and frank engagement by stakeholders and other interested parties in the development of criminal justice policy. The seminar series was held as the criminal justice bill was passing through parliament, and in an obvious sense the policies incorporated into the bill had already been established. However, the bill's passage, through the House of Lords in particular, was controversial and keenly contested, and it was not finally completed until mid-November 2003. In fact, Royal Assent was not secured until, literally, minutes before the end of the 2002/3 parliamentary session. Furthermore, even as the bill was being discussed, the government was planning further criminal justice legislation, including a victims' bill to be introduced in the next parliamentary session.[13] In order to provide a forum for informed discussion that might, at least, be taken into account in the future development of policy, delegates were invited from the key ministries, particularly the Home Office and the Department for Constitutional Affairs (which replaced the Lord Chancellor's Department during the course of the seminar series). Also invited were stakeholders such as prosecution and defence lawyers, those representing victims' groups such as Victim Support, together with academics and others.

Criminal justice under Labour

The Labour government elected in 1997 made criminal justice one of its key policy areas, and it has outstripped any previous government in the amount and compass of legislative and other initiatives concerning crime, criminal processes and public order. This phenomenon has been noted and examined elsewhere,[14] and will not be

---

13 The domestic violence, crime and victims bill was published on 2 December 2003. See the Home Office press release CJSO11/2003 issued on 2 December 2003 which described the rationale of the bill as being 'the Government's commitment to putting victims at the heart of the criminal justice system'.

14 See, for example, Tonry, above, n10, D. Downes and R. Morgan, 'The skeletons in the cupboard: the politics of law and order at the turn of the millennium', in M. Maguire et al (eds), *The Oxford Handbook of Criminology*, (3rd ed, Oxford University Press, 2002), and T. Jones and T. Newburn, 'The convergence of US and UK crime control policy: exploring substance and process', in T. Newburn and R. Sparks, *Criminal Justice and Political Cultures*, (Willan, 2004).

further explored here, but before considering some of the issues raised in the papers presented at the seminars it is worth stating a few basic facts about crime and criminal justice policy to provide a context for what follows.

The crime rate in England and Wales has broadly declined over the past ten years, and the latest Home Office figures show that the chances of being a victim of crime are now about the same as they were in 1981.[15] On the other hand, the prison population, at around 74,000, is nearly double what it was a decade ago. Tonry describes the 'record and rising' prison population as a remarkable phenomenon because, he says, it has occurred during a period of generally declining crime rates, and 'no plausible case can be made that a long-term increase in the imprisonment rate or enactment of tougher sentencing laws led to the decline in crime rates'.[16] The prison population has been rapidly rising despite the fact that crime has been reducing; the increased use by the courts of custodial sentences is not the cause of the declining crime rate.

With regard to victims the government has, since coming to office, introduced a series of initiatives designed to improve the position and experience of victims of crime, some of which built on policies initiated by the previous Conservative government. It has, for example, introduced a national telephone helpline, and support services for victims and witnesses in magistrates' courts, provided through Victim Support. A personal victim statement scheme was introduced nationally in 2001 following a series of pilot projects. Victims of certain serious crimes have been given the right to be consulted about the release plans of 'their' offenders and, as noted by John Spencer and John Jackson in this volume, the government has introduced 'special measures' for vulnerable witnesses (including victims) when giving evidence.[17]

It is difficult to identify any initiatives since the present Labour government came to power (and for some years prior to that) that have been designed to improve the rights of persons suspected of or accused of crime. It is true that the introduction of the Human Rights Act 1998 was expected by many to have a positive impact on the position of suspects and defendants but, in the event, the effects have

---

15 See *Crime in England and Wales Quarterly Update to September 2003*, HO Bulletin 03/04, Home Office, London, 22 January 2004.

16 See Tonry, n10, at p3.

17 For a government account of its policies on victims see *A Better Deal for Victims and Witnesses*, Home Office Communications Directorate, November 2002.

been relatively muted in this respect.[18] It is also the case that expenditure on criminal legal aid is at an all time high,[19] but this has hardly been the result of deliberate policy decisions.[20] The means test for criminal legal aid was abolished in 2001 but that was done principally because collecting contributions was uneconomic and led to inefficiencies in the progress of cases.[21] Against this, significant limitations have been imposed on the presumption of innocence by the 'abolition' of the 'right to silence'[22] and the obligation of the defence to serve a defence statement.[23] The police and the prosecution, on the other hand, have seen their powers and resources, and their influence over government policy, increase inexorably over the past decade or so. Many, including participants in the recent Cambridge crime policy conference[24] believe that any imbalance between prosecution and defence unfairly favours the former rather than the latter.[25]

What is criminal justice for?

In order to understand the (actual and possible) relationship between victims' and defendants' rights it is helpful to consider the purpose(s) of the criminal justice system. Such a question can be considered at different levels of abstraction and a number of the speakers made reference, in particular, to the recent influential work of David Garland, *The Culture of Control,*[26] in which he argues that the significant changes to criminal justice policy since the early 1990s, including

18 See, for example, A. Ashworth, *Human Rights, Serious Crime and Criminal Procedure,* (Sweet and Maxwell, 2002).

19 See the Legal Services Commission Annual Report 2002/03, HC743, TSO, London, 2003.

20 In June 2003 the Lord Chancellor's Department issued a consultation paper *Delivering value for money in the Criminal Defence Service* which proposed to revise the scope of the criminal legal aid scheme in order to bring spending under control. On 2 February 2004 David Lammy, the minister responsible for legal aid, confirmed a significant reduction in scope of the criminal legal aid scheme would be implemented.

21 A Criminal Defence Service Bill which, amongst other things, is expected to re-introduce the means test, is due to be published in Spring 2004.

22 Criminal Justice and Public Order Act 1994 ss34–38, and see A. Ashworth, *The Criminal Process* (2nd ed, Oxford University Press, 1998), p96.

23 Criminal Procedure and Investigations Act 1996 ss5 and 6.

24 See n10.

25 See Tonry, n10, at p235.

26 See n12.

governments' attitude to victims of crime, can only be understood in the context of a rapidly changing social environment. In her chapter, Walklate uses this as a basis for an analysis of the changing context of criminal justice policy in which government has been replaced by governance, and the managerialist agenda of New Labour has altered the notion of the 'public interest' and gone for a 'quick fix' approach to social problems.

The government, unsurprisingly, takes an essentially pragmatic view – the criminal justice system has two specific aims: to reduce crime and the fear of crime and their social and economic consequences; and to dispense justice fairly and efficiently, promoting confidence in the rule of law.[27] Of course, articulation by a government of what it regards as the purpose of the criminal justice system is quite different from a philosophical or sociological analysis of what criminal justice systems and processes are for, and what functions they fulfil. It is to be expected, therefore, that Paul Clark appears to speak a different 'language' in this respect from some of the other contributors. Nevertheless, Walklate's proposition that 'respect' is a fundamental need of human beings, including victims and defendants, serves as an important yardstick by which both the government's aims and its criminal justice policies can be assessed. Further, Hudson reminds us that historically the main dichotomy was between the state and the victim and it may be that whilst the focus has shifted to the relationship between victims and defendants, this obscures a continuing tension between state and victim. As Ashworth has argued,[28] the state needs victims – to report crimes, to provide information, to give evidence – and they are more likely to serve this function if they have confidence in the system; a point implicitly accepted by Clark and reflected in the government's policy pamphlet *A Better Deal for Victims and Witnesses* which states that '[w]itnesses[29] are essential to the success of the entire criminal justice system and they should be treated on that basis'.[30] Thus 'promoting confidence in the rule of law' serves instrumental purposes of the state, but policies designed to promote the confidence of victims may sit uneasily with fairness for defendants, an issue not addressed by the government.

27 See *A Guide to the Criminal Justice System in England and Wales*, Home Office, 2000.

28 A. Ashworth, 'Victims' rights, defendants' rights and criminal procedure' in A. Crawford and J. Goodey (eds), *Integrating a Victim Perspective Within Criminal Justice*, (Ashgate, 2000).

29 And all victims are potential or actual witnesses.

30 See n17.

A second-order question is what are criminal proceedings for? This is the question posed by John Spencer, and he answers it by differentiating between primary and secondary aims. The primary aim is to convict and punish the guilty and acquit the innocent. The secondary aim is to ensure, in carrying out the primary aim, that as little pain as possible is caused to everyone concerned. It follows, says Spencer, that the accused must be at the centre of the proceedings. As Jackson notes, the risks of injustice are not the same, that is, not so serious for victims as for defendants. The government continues to state that it accepts the primary aim: 'The most fundamental [principles are] that someone is innocent until proved guilty and that the prosecution must prove its case against the defendant beyond reasonable doubt. If a reasonable doubt remains, the defendant is unquestionably entitled to the benefit of it'.[31] Clark appears to accept this, but is dissatisfied with a system which, he says, is 'built around the defendant'. This reflects government thinking. The government is committed to 'putting victims at the heart of the criminal justice system' said Lord Falconer in welcoming the publication of the domestic violence, crime and victims bill.[32] If this is more than a rhetorical flourish the government could not accept Spencer's secondary aim as being subsidiary to the first, at least as far as victims are concerned. The conflicts and tensions inherent in such a position are left unaddressed by Clark or the government.

One further, related, issue is the characterisation of the criminal trial as a game in which the rules are designed to give defendants 'a sporting chance' of getting off, used as a further justification for the assertion that trials are inappropriately centred on defendants. Paul Clark refers to the report of Lord Justice Auld in which, in fact, he emphatically states that 'the criminal process is not a game'.[33] The analogy is also used in disapproving terms in *Justice for All*: 'the system should not become a game where delay and obstruction can be used as a tactic to avoid a rightful conviction'.[34] Hickman, by contrast, believes that trials should be treated as a game, not because they are frivolous or unimportant, but because game-playing is a fundamentally human activity: 'parties and their lawyers will always seek to manipulate any set of rules to their best advantage'. This has to be right and, contrary to the government's representation of the issue, it

31 See *Justice for All*, n7, at p69.
32 See the Home Office press release CJSO11/2003, issued on 2 December 2003.
33 *Review of the Criminal Courts of England and Wales*, n12, at p11.
34 n7, p16.

is not only defendants and their lawyers who use rules to further their interests. The proper response, says Hickman, is to recognise this and to provide a fair framework and adequate resources 'to both sides'. A question that this begs is whether the victim is to be treated as being on one of the sides, or as some category of third party, although Hickman's approach could be accommodated within the conception of the role of victims in some inquisitorial systems, referred to by both Clark and Sanders.

Fair trial?

One of the tests of whether the government is serious when it states that it regards fair trial for those accused of crime as a fundamental principle is to examine the rationale for and practical consequences and implications of actual and proposed changes to the criminal trial process. If, as is suggested above, the government has failed to address the conflicts inherent in placing victims at the heart of the process, one would expect to see defendants being unduly prejudiced in the process of such re-positioning. Further, if the argument put forward by many of the speakers, that 'victim' is a political construct that is used for purposes other than providing for the real needs of real victims, one would expect to see that such changes, whilst prejudicing defendants, do not necessarily satisfy victims' needs or interests. These questions are addressed, directly or indirectly, in most of the chapters in this book, but whilst the government has provided a rationalisation for changes such as those in the criminal justice bill – that is, they serve the interests of victims and the community – it has generally failed to engage with the concerns about the consequences and implications. This disengagement is evident in Clark's chapter. For example, he sidesteps the research evidence that knowledge of a defendant's previous misconduct may prejudice a jury or magistrates by simply asserting that the bill would permit such evidence to be admitted only 'where this is relevant to the case and provided there isn't [an] adverse effect on the fairness of the proceedings'. There is no indication of an awareness of the questions this begs, nor an acknowledgement that the bill only gave a partial discretion to courts to exclude such evidence.[35] Spencer makes the point that not all changes that are detrimental to the interests of defendants are necessarily inimical to

---

35 Clause 84(3) of the bill as originally published gave the court a discretion to exclude evidence of bad character only where it was admitted for some, but not all, of the purposes set out in cl84(1). See now Criminal Justice Act 2003 s101(3).

fair trial. Having established the primary aims of the criminal trial he says that it is legitimate to ask two questions in respect of defendants' rights: do they contribute to the court reaching a just result? Do they contribute to the civilised conduct of proceedings? In respect of any particular change in existing rights, the proper question, Spencer argues, is not whether it would weaken the rights of defendants, but whether it would weaken their position in any way that undermines the main objectives of criminal proceedings. He then uses this analytical method to assess recent changes (but not those in the criminal justice bill) that were designed to improve the position of victims. Most, according to Spencer, do not offend the requirement that they should not undermine the twin objectives, although some are not very effective and others, especially 'special measures' under the Youth Justice and Criminal Evidence Act 1999, are not even-handed since they are not available to vulnerable defendant witnesses; an assessment with which Jackson broadly agrees.

What of the provisions in the criminal justice bill? Clark concentrates on the evidential provisions regarding previous misconduct and hearsay, the new charging arrangements, and retrial following acquittal in serious cases.[36] Whilst it would not be reasonable to expect him to have addressed all of the major provisions of the bill, it is notable that he ignored the increase in police powers in Part 1, and the disclosure provisions that place a heavy, and unequal, burden on the accused. As Jackson comments in respect of the defence disclosure provisions, 'even as a balancing exercise the proposal appears flawed'. With regard to the provisions that Clark does refer to, he argues that they are beneficial for victims in a number of ways. The existing restrictions on the admission of evidence are confusing and difficult to apply, and prevent effective testimony being given by witnesses. They encourage game-playing by the defence and deter witnesses from giving evidence.

The new charging arrangements, which transfer responsibility for charge decisions from the police to the Crown Prosecution Service, have very little connection with the other changes cited by Clark and are neutral as between accused and victim. In respect of the other provisions he refers to, what Clark does not do – and this is also true of *Justice for All* – is to pay any heed to the reasons why the rules on hearsay, previous misconduct and double jeopardy were developed. It is as if they were invented solely to facilitate game-playing and to frustrate the proper purpose of criminal trials. In ignoring the history

36 See now Parts 11, 4 and 10 respectively of the Criminal Justice Act 2003.

of these rules, Clark and the government fail to engage with the very real concerns that such changes undermine Spencer's twin objectives. As Jackson argues, the provisions wrongly assume that the issues at stake are the same for victims as they are for the accused, and consequently disadvantage the defence but also jeopardise the chances of fair trial.

As an example of the disingenuous approach of the government, take the provisions on evidence of previous misconduct of the accused which were far from even-handed as between the accused and other witnesses. Although the government gave the impression that they were implementing the recommendations of the Law Commission, the provisions in the bill as published went far further than the Commission's recommendations. In *Justice for All* the government acknowledged the research that demonstrates that both juries and magistrates are unduly prejudiced by knowledge of a defendant's previous convictions and stated '[t]hat is why we are opposed to the routine introduction of all previous convictions as evidence in a case'.[37] However, the Explanatory Notes issued with the Bill when it was published explained that the relevant clauses 'provide an inclusionary approach to a defendant's previous convictions and other misconduct'.[38] That the bill provided for the almost routine admission of evidence of previous convictions was certainly the conclusion drawn by the Home Affairs Committee, who went on to say that 'we believe that these provisions could lead to miscarriages of justice in some cases. In particular, we are concerned at the prospect of using a defendant's previous record to prop up what might otherwise be a weak case. We are also concerned that this will increase the temptation for the police to pursue the "usual suspects"'.[39] As Klug observes, '[I]t is difficult to entirely remove the suspicion that [these provisions are] rather more about increasing clear-up rates . . . than increasing the protection of individuals from violent crime'. It should be remembered that the government has set a target of increasing the clear-up rate by about 20 per cent in five years from 2000/1.[40]

37 See *Justice for All*, n7, at p80. For the research evidence see *Evidence in Criminal Proceedings*, n12, Appendix D para D.63, and S. Lloyd-Bostock, 'The effects on juries of hearing about the defendant's previous criminal record: a simulation study' [2000] Crim LR 734.

38 See *Criminal Justice Bill Explanatory Notes* Bill 8-EN, TSO, London, 21 November 2002, para 298.

39 House of Commons Home Affairs Committee, Criminal Justice Bill, Second Report of Session 2002-03, HC 83, TSO, London, 2002, para 116.

40 *Narrowing the Justice Gap*, October 2002, p3, available at www.cjsonline.gov.uk/njg/documents/njg-framework.pdf.

What rights should victims have?

All of the speakers, directly or by implication, addressed the question of what rights victims should have, although Sanders argues that they should not have rights at all, at least not in a legal sense. All agree that victims' interests are not adequately catered for at present in England and Wales, and one area of agreement between Clark and Sanders is that the opportunities for victim participation in some systems with an inquisitorial tradition may provide significant benefits for victims. Reflecting Walklate's notion of respect, and Hudson's call for a more discursive approach, Sanders argues that victims' 'understanding is increased through participation, dialogue and sight of the material on the basis of which decisions are made', and greater understanding is likely to increase perceptions of legitimacy and acceptance of outcomes that are otherwise regarded as unjust. It is relevant to note, in this regard, that recent Home Office sponsored research demonstrates that participation in the criminal process by serving on juries increases people's understanding of, and general satisfaction with, the trial process.[41]

I intend to deal here with two aspects of the debate. The first concerns human rights and the perception that human rights norms, and the European Convention on Human Rights (ECHR) in particular, ignore victims of crime. Francesca Klug castigates human rights lawyers for focusing on defendants' and prisoners' rights, 'victims' of the state, to the exclusion of victims of crime: 'In this Alice in Wonderland world it is not difficult for the Home Secretary to play the part of the Queen of Hearts and shout "off with their heads" every time he spots a lawyer or judge'. She argues that victims are, and should be, at the heart of human rights concerns and calls for a refocusing of human rights discourse.

As Klug acknowledges, the human rights approach will not normally provide clear-cut answers, but it can provide a framework within which competing claims can be assessed. This approach is particularly useful where the respective claims relate to rights that are of a different order of significance: Ashworth distinguishes between 'absolute', 'strong' and 'prima facie' rights.[42] For example, the right

---

41 See R. Matthews, L. Hancock and D. Briggs, *Jurors' perceptions, understanding, confidence and satisfaction in the jury system: a study in six courts*, Home Office, London, 2004, available online at www.homeoffice.gov.uk/rds/pdfs2/r.227.pdf.

42 See A. Ashworth, n22, ch2. See also K. Starmer, *European Human Rights Law*, (LAG, 1999), who distinguishes between absolute, derogable and qualified rights.

not to be subjected to torture, inhuman or degrading treatment (art 3 ECHR) should normally carry greater weight than the right to fair trial (art 6). It is more difficult to apply where the competing interests are located within rights of the same order of significance, such as the right to liberty and security (art 5) and the right to fair trial.[43] That is not to say that in such circumstances the human rights approach is of no value. In *Doorson v Netherlands*, for example, the European Court of Human Rights was willing to endorse measures designed to protect witnesses even though they had adverse implications for the right of the accused to confront witnesses under article 6(3)(d).[44]

However, despite Klug's powerful argument for a reconceptualisation of victims rights within human rights discourse, significant difficulties remain within the current framework which she appears to acknowledge when she states that victims 'are (*or should be*) central to human rights thinking' (emphasis added). First, as Klug reminds us, international law generally, and the ECHR in particular, is principally concerned with the relationship between individuals and the state, and not with relationships between individuals. The Convention itself does not contain explicit rights for victims of crime in the way that it does contain rights explicitly directed at those accused of crime, and the jurisprudence on the obligations of the state to protect individuals against infringement of their rights by other individuals is relatively under-developed. Second, as Klug also reminds us, victims of crime are not conceived of as an interest group, and this is reflected in the fact that whilst there is a corpus of criminal defence lawyers who represent a clear interest group, there is no similar corpus of 'victims' lawyers'. Third, the government's representation of victims' interests reinforces the notion that victims of crime have quite separate interests from victims of the state and corporate bodies.

The second aspect of the debate to be considered here is the specific argument over victim impact statements (VIS). Two notable protagonists, Edna Erez and Andrew Sanders, both of whom have conducted extensive research in this area, set out their respective positions in the third seminar, and in their chapters in this book. Erez argues that the criminal justice system should serve the 'perceived justice needs' of victims and promote their psychological welfare. Victim input at the sentencing stage is beneficial to victims, reducing

---

43   A similar point is made by Sanders and Young. See A. Sanders and R. Young, *Criminal Justice*, (2nd ed, Butterworths, 2000), p34.

44   (1996) 22 EHRR 330, and see the discussion in A. Ashworth, *Human rights, Serious Crime and Criminal Procedure*, (Sweet and Maxwell, 2002), p77.

trauma and increasing their overall satisfaction with the process. The most significant goal of victims is public recognition of their status as a victim. The problem, she says, is that in response to opposition by the legal profession, VIS have been refashioned as a potential aid to sentencing rather than being a mechanism for providing 'victim voice'. Thus diverted from their true purpose, research has been misinterpreted in order to support objections to victims' input at sentencing.

Sanders, although expressing it in different language, accepts that participation is potentially beneficial for victims, but argues that VIS is not the route to effective participation. Whatever the 'true' purpose of VIS, it inevitably comes to be inextricably linked to sentencing and this, research in the United Kingdom and elsewhere demonstrates, is likely to lead to more, not less, dissatisfaction. Why is this? Sanders' research found that many victims believed that their VIS had been ignored and although this was not the case in the sense that judges, prosecutors and others had taken no notice of them, few VIS had made any perceptible difference to sentence or other relevant decisions. For Sanders this is structural and inevitable. Most cases are routine in the sense that the impact of the crime on the victim is what would be expected, but when victims' statements indicated that the impact had been out of the ordinary, 'they had to be "taken with a pinch of salt" in the absence of supporting evidence'.[45]

There is a level of agreement between Erez and Sanders. Erez emphasises the restorative function of VIS as a 'mechanism for victim voice', and Sanders accepts the restorative functions of victim involvement. However, they diverge on the solutions to increasing victims' participation. In many respects, Sanders' approach is the more radical of the two. Whilst Erez argues for providing 'voice' by allowing victims to write their own statements and present them in person to the court, unmediated by the police or by legal professionals, Sanders argues for more effective participation by adapting features of inquisitorial systems which allow for greater participation, dialogue and knowledge of relevant material.

---

45 The Consolidated Criminal Practice Direction [2002] 3 All ER 904, [2002] 1 WLR 2870. Part III para 28.2 provides that 'Except where inferences can properly be drawn from the nature or of circumstances surrounding the offence, a sentencer must not make assumptions unsupported by evidence about the effects of an offence on the victim'.

Balance and reconciliation

Where Erez and Sanders fundamentally disagree is on the implications of VIS for the 'balance' between victims' and defendants' rights.
Erez argues that research demonstrates that generally victims are not
interested in changing sentence decisions, and that victim impact
statements do not increase sentence severity. Sanders' research, on
the other hand, demonstrates that over half of victims in his sample
who made a VIS did so for an instrumental purpose, which included
increasing the severity of sentence.[46] Thus Sanders concludes that
victim impact statements are detrimental to defendants' interests,
without providing any advantage – instrumental or expressive – to
victims. Erez, by contrast, concludes that VIS produce no necessary
conflict between the respective interests of victims and defendants,
and that 'they may even be compatible in regards to its *restorative
justice* aims' [emphasis added]. A problem for Erez, of course, is that
the restorative justice aims of VIS do not necessarily coincide with the
aims or interests of defendants. Furthermore, in England and Wales
at least, VIS are not confined to providing a mechanism for 'victim
voice' because the scheme explicitly envisages that they may be taken
into account in determining sentence.[47]

Spencer argues that giving victims the opportunity to have an
input at the sentencing stage does not undermine the legitimate interests of defendants since it does not undermine the twin aims of criminal proceedings. Similarly, Sanders argues that victim involvement
in sentencing does not involve a clash of rights, although it does raise
the question of whether it is an appropriate way of doing justice, both
for defendants and for victims. This raises an important empirical
question, which is whether VIS do contribute to the appropriate punishment of those found guilty. Extrapolating from her research on
offenders, Hudson suggests that VIS may have an unintended effect
on sentences as a result of differential attitudes to particular victims
and defendants resulting from their personal and social characteristics, such as ethnic origin. Both Erez and Sanders have some difficulty
with the question. Erez argues that VIS do not necessarily lead to more
severe sentences, but that VIS are not (and should not be) principally
concerned with affecting sentence in any event. Sanders argues
that VIS are highly unlikely to lead to less severe sentences (except,

46 See A. Sanders et al, 'Victim Impact Statements: don't work, can't work', [2001]
    Crim LR 447, at p450.
47 The Consolidated Criminal Practice Direction, n45, Part III para 28.1.

possibly, in the context of restorative justice approaches), but that in practice VIS are generally ignored, and that forcing sentencers to explain any effect of a VIS on them is likely to lead to more dissatisfaction for victims.

The VIS scheme in England and Wales was rolled out nationally despite the evidence from the pilot project that they were not a satisfactory way of providing victims with greater satisfaction and confidence.[48] It was a 'fudge' and a quick fix when what was needed was something more fundamental. Defendants' interests, if not their rights, were potentially compromised without providing any significant benefit for victims. This is a theme that goes right to the core of the debate. Whilst 'service rights' for victims – being kept informed about the progress of cases and decisions made, counselling and support, etc – are uncontroversial in terms of the victim/defendant dichotomy, there has been a marked lack of commitment and resources to make them work satisfactorily – although recent government announcements may signal a change. Procedural rights for victims, including VIS, are often easier and cheaper to implement than service rights, but they do have the potential to adversely affect defendants' legitimate interests. As Sanders notes in his chapter, there are genuinely hard cases. He points to the restrictions on the use of sexual history evidence introduced by the Youth Justice and Criminal Evidence Act 1999. The problem is that in such cases, governments tend to ignore the potential for undermining defendants' rights. Other procedural rights, such as the 'special measures' provisions applicable to vulnerable witnesses introduced by the same Act, may have less profound implications for defendants' rights[49] but are simply unfair if, as Spencer and Jackson point out, they are not even handed as between victims (and other witnesses) and defendants. It is the responsibility of governments in respect of such measures to carefully consider the implications for fair trial, to ensure that they do not inappropriately discriminate between victims and defendants, and to ensure that they are carefully implemented and monitored. What is important is how they affect real defendants and real victims in real trials.

The criminal justice bill was not, for the most part, concerned with either service rights or procedural rights for victims. The controversial provisions referred to by Paul Clark, those concerning previous

---

48 See A. Sanders et al, n46.

49 Although this will depend upon the detail of the provisions and how they are implemented in actual trials.

misconduct, hearsay and re-trial following acquittal were, in Jackson's terms, 'outcome-related measures' designed to increase the number of convictions. One might also add to this list the provisions on defence disclosure since in practice, if not in principle, they are likely to lead to fewer defendants being able to put forward a successful defence. These do undermine the legitimate rights of defendants. Whilst they may well increase the number of convictions, the evidence suggests that this will be at the expense of some innocent defendants being convicted. In respect of provisions of this kind it is not a question of reconciling rights. Reducing the rights of defendants in such a way that increases the chances of innocent people being convicted does nothing to enhance the rights or interests of victims. The problem is that the government, in appealing to victims' rights to justify its criminal justice policies, denies certain real tensions between the interests of victims and defendants, obscures others, and uses victims for purposes that have nothing to do with their real interests. Why they do this has more to do with the crisis of post-modern governance than with any crisis in criminal justice.

CHAPTER 2

Redressing the balance: the criminal justice bill 2002

By Paul Clark

Member of Parliament for Gillingham and Assistant Government Whip

Let me at the start thank you for providing an opportunity for the government to give its view at the beginning of this series of important seminars.[1] I am no lawyer and yet I am a constituency Member of Parliament, who invariably has people coming to me out of sheer desperation when they feel that the criminal justice system is letting them down and failing to protect them as 'honest' citizens.

Ten or so years ago, talk of victims' rights had barely reached the margins of anyone's thinking. The first Victim's Charter was not published until 1990. It was not until the second Charter in 1996 that the criminal justice agencies began to take their responsibilities seriously on a national level, however good practices may have been in some parts of the country. Yet here we are just a few years later talking about the possibility of victims' rights.

We are taking this step now because our criminal justice system is not working as well as it could, or as well as it needs to, to address the needs of victims. It is an inefficient system in which too many people escape justice, and the public lack confidence. It lacks that public confidence because of the examples that follow[2] and because the facts speak for themselves.

---

1 Paul Clark MP was speaking as PPS to the Secretary of State for Constitutional Affairs, Lord Falconer.
2 Home Office Statistics.

- Nearly a quarter of defendants commit at least one offence on bail. Juveniles were more than twice as likely than adults to offend on bail.
- 12 per cent of those bailed fail to appear at court.
- In 1999, 25 per cent of ineffective trails in the Crown Court and 19 per cent of ineffective trails in the Magistrates' courts were due to witness non-attendance.
- It is estimated that 30,000 cases were abandoned in 2001 because witnesses and victims refused to give evidence in court or failed to turn up.
- The British Crime Survey found only 46 per cent of people are confident that the system is effective in bringing criminals to justice and only 1 in 4 are confident that the CJS meets the needs of victims.

It is against this background of inefficiency and lack of public confidence that we all must act.

To protect themselves against the might of the state, suspects are given important rights, and safeguards to regulate how they are treated, at every stage of the process, and often receive free and highly skilled legal representation.

I am not criticising this. In many ways, it is something to be proud of. It should mean there are fewer people convicted of crimes they did not commit. We do not want to see a return to the miscarriages of justice of the 1970s – the Guildford Four, the Birmingham Six, Judith Ward, and the particularly tragic case of Stefan Kisko. The problems with confession evidence and the lack of systematic disclosure by the then prosecution clearly had to be put right.

PACE and, much more recently, the provisions of the ECHR are welcome safeguards, but it has led to a view that everything has been done for the offender and little has been done for the victim. It is a view with which I have considerable sympathy.

I am reminded of an incident which I had witnessed of dangerous driving, which almost led to a fatality. I had provided the police with a statement as did other witnesses, and I also had the index number of the vehicle involved. The due date came to appear at court as a witness. This in itself was daunting. An unfamiliar place, a language used that is shrouded in mystery, procedures that seem arcane. A whole day booked off work to do my duty. After three hours of waiting, I am dismissed. Why, because the defendant did not turn up. And I never did get recalled.

As a Member of Parliament, people have come to my advice surgery confused, angry, ignorant, through no fault of their own, as to an incident, a case with which they have had some involvement – only to feel let down and frustrated by the system. How many times have I heard residents say 'we know John is the ringleader – he's been picked up by the police so many times – but nothing happens'. Or 'I've told the police who it is – I saw them. But I've told them that I won't go to court, because they will pick on me and the next thing I'll have a brick through the window.' And it is against this background that we, as a Government, launched our programme of reform, with the *Justice for All* White Paper last summer.

Justice for All is guided by a single clear priority – to rebalance the criminal justice system in favour of the victim and the community so as to reduce crime and to bring offenders to justice. I want to shift the perception, which Sir Robin Auld referred to in his *Review of the Criminal Courts*, that a criminal trial is a game in which a guilty defendant should be provided with a sporting chance of getting off.

There are too many restrictions on the evidence which courts may hear and there are also too many technical rules preventing the effective testimony of witnesses. We believe that the widest range of evidence should be available to juries that will enable them to reach a just verdict.

The current rules are confusing and difficult to apply. They encourage defendants and lawyers to view the criminal justice system as a game and can dissuade witnesses from testifying for fear of having their character attacked in court or the process becoming one of secondary victimisation. The reforms in our criminal justice bill, now in the Second Chamber, will enable judges to let juries hear about a defendant's previous convictions and other misconduct where this is relevant to the case and provided there isn't an adverse affect on the fairness of the proceedings.

Another rule addressed in the bill is that which prevents hearsay statements from being used in criminal proceedings. Both legal practitioners and academics have consistently called for reform of the hearsay rule and its exceptions, which are confusing to operate and waste court time. There is a lack of consistency in the way judges exercise their discretion, and some – perhaps those with a traditional hostility to hearsay – regularly prevent hearsay statements from being used. But the biggest problem with this rule is that cogent evidence is arbitrarily excluded (even if it is evidence which points to the innocence of the accused), no matter how reliable and convincing the evidence involved.

Under our reforms in the criminal justice bill, there will be a comprehensive scheme to replace complex and inconsistent rules; evidence will automatically be admitted in some cases (providing greater certainty for practitioners about when out of court statements can be used); judges will have the power to admit other relevant evidence, (subject to safeguards to ensure a fair trial); and these reforms will assist witnesses to give evidence – their testimony is more likely to help in finding the truth, rather than be a test of long term memory.[3] We are introducing a number of other practical measures to benefit victims and witnesses as well as the justice process itself.

Over the last few months we have been piloting new charging arrangements where the CPS has responsibility from the outset for determining charges in most cases. The indications are encouraging. Cases where the evidence is weak are identified earlier. This gives the police the chance to obtain further evidence so the case can proceed or, if there is no likelihood of a successful prosecution, the investigation can be abandoned at an early stage. It enables the police to receive advice from prosecutors on what they know from their courtroom experience is likely to be convincing evidence.[4]

For victims and witnesses, there are fewer raised and then dashed expectations as they are no longer told one thing by the police and then another by the CPS. Reducing delay in bringing cases before the courts brings clear benefits for victims and witnesses as well as for the administration of justice itself. It increases the likelihood that witnesses will not drop out of the case before it gets before the court. Or that they are forever turning up and told they are not required that day. Add to that the possibility that they may be fearful of the defendant or his supporters, or just the understandable anxiety of being cross-examined by a clever lawyer, and there is a clear recipe for witnesses dropping out.

Contrary to some reports, we don't want to do anything about clever lawyers. But we can and are taking steps to ensure that cases are heard when they are supposed to be heard. And that witnesses only turn up if they are needed, and have somewhere safe to wait before giving evidence – away from the court buildings with a mobile phone if necessary. The lessons we have learned from the Street Crime Initiative, which will be taken forward in other pilot sites around the country, will also contribute to the development of future good practices.

3   See now Criminal Justice Act 2003 Pt 11, Ch 2.
4   This scheme is facilitated by Criminal Justice Act 2003 Pt 4 and Sch 2.

Our plan to abolish the double jeopardy rule also contributes. Why should those who have been wrongly acquitted of the most serious offences be able to feel as if they have got away with it. How would we feel if we had had a child murdered and convincing new scientific evidence came to light which could convict the offender – except that he had already been found not guilty of the offence and so nothing more could be done. Any reasonable person would regard this as a gross miscarriage of justice.[5]

As well as these changes to the process, there are overt measures we can take to provide a better framework for delivering services to victims and witnesses. As I mentioned above, we shall be honouring our manifesto commitment to introduce a victims' bill during the course of this Parliament.[6] At its heart will be a power for the Home Secretary to introduce a Victims' Code of Practice, binding on all the criminal justice agencies, committing them to provide specific services, within challenging deadlines, on issues such as the provision of information, protection and support. This will be a significant improvement on the current Victim's Charter. To police this Code of Practice we will introducing an explicit avenue of complaint to the Parliamentary Ombudsman so that individual cases can be taken up.

We will also establish a Commissioner for Victims and Witnesses to ensure not only that the procedures we put in place have the intended benefit but also to comment more widely on how government departments and agencies respond to the needs of victims and witnesses – to give deeper thought to their health, housing, social security and, where children and young people are concerned, their educational needs. A primary role for the commissioner is to raise awareness of victims issues and represent their interests to government and the public.

We have a firm commitment to extend specialised support services for victims of road traffic incidents, which we highlighted in *Justice for All*[7] and *A better deal for victims and witnesses*.[8] The untimely loss of a loved one in a road traffic accident causes untold grief, no more so when it is through another's careless or drunken driving. We are establishing pilot projects in number of areas to test approaches to providing support, identify good practice in meeting victims' needs and form conclusions on the best likely model for national use. These

5 See now Criminal Justice Act 2003 Pt 10.
6 The domestic violence, crime and victim bill was published 2 December 2003.
7 Cm 5563.
8 Home Office Communication Directorate, November 2002.

pilots will build on in-depth review of specialist support available to people bereaved by road death conducted last autumn.

And there has been other recent encouraging progress – for example, all police forces in England and Wales will routinely deploy police family liaison officers for all fatal road traffic incidents and the CPS will undertake a thematic review of services for road crash victims.

These are all important developments, and are in hand. But are we doing enough to acknowledge the role of victims in court proceedings?

In this country, the personal support they receive before the trial – from the voluntary organisation Victim Support – is second to none. So, why does the victim have no direct role in the trial unless they are a witness giving evidence? Because the whole system is built around the defendant, so the victim feels at best ignored and at worst victimised again. Shouldn't we be asking what effect the trial has on the victim – or their family in murder cases? Do they feel that justice has been done? Do they feel that their voice has been listened to? Do they feel they have a voice at all? Yes, we now have a written victim statement scheme which enables them to say how the crime has affected them. But does this go far enough in putting their interests at the heart of the criminal justice system?

The Home Secretary has recently set up a Victims Advisory Panel, which is chaired by Lord Falconer. In the main, it is made up of the victims of very serious crimes, or their bereaved relatives in murder cases. On other occasions, Home Office ministers have had one-off meetings with those who have been seriously victimised. The message these victims convey is that the police were generally helpful and supportive; the Crown Prosecution Service has got better; that they are thankful for the introduction of victim statements; and that they are pleased that they can have a say when the release plans of offenders are being considered. But they have very little good to say about the trial itself.

Can we learn from how other jurisdictions treat victims, particularly those with a non-adversarial system? Some in the legal establishment would regard that question as at best heretical, at worst treasonable.

I am not an expert in other European jurisdictions. But, I know that in France, for example, under the *partie civile* procedure, the victim is entitled to present a claim for compensation to the court as part of the criminal trial and can put questions to witnesses and experts to substantiate the claim. The French inquisitorial system is more concerned with getting to the truth of the crime which has been committed, rather than which side's lawyer is able to put forward the most persuasive argument.

In other parts of Europe – in Germany or Austria for example – the victim has the opportunity to become assistant or auxiliary prosecutor. Depending on the circumstances of the particular case, the victim can then:

- be informed of the date of all hearings and attend them;
- have the chance of being seated next to the public prosecutor;
- put questions to witnesses, or suggest that the prosecutor asks a particular question;
- make oral statements to the court.

Are some of these measures possible to import without undermining our criminal justice system or without attacking judicial discretion?

I am not suggesting of course that victims should be allowed to make direct and unfiltered interventions in proceedings in front of a jury. But their claims for compensation for damages or loss – when they are not already covered by our state compensation scheme – should be put more rigorously by the prosecuting lawyer, in consultation with victims. A guaranteed seat next to the prosecutor is an important symbolic step. The defendant handing notes to his solicitor during the course of a trial is a familiar sight. Why shouldn't the victim have the same opportunity if it leads to a greater prospect of justice?

It is in the interests of the state, which the prosecutor would continue to represent, to have all the available information before it. Even more so after a defendant has pleaded guilty or been found guilty. How often do we then hear a plea in mitigation, particularly after a plea of guilt, in which aspersions are cast on the victim's character or behaviour. They too often go unchallenged because the victim does not have the opportunity to tell the prosecutor that a tissue of lies is being put forward.

These are small but important ways in which we can improve the experience of criminal proceedings for victims. They may not be in our legislative programme at present, and more discussion and consultation is required on the detail, but I should like to think that in another five to ten years' time it will be taken for granted that victims are an integral part of the process.

That is one of the things that our system can do better, and make a big difference not only to victims' lives, but in the confidence of others to come forward and report crime. They will know that they will be supported from start to end of the process, and afterwards too if they wish. There will not suddenly be a gap in care and concern as soon as they set foot in the court room.

These are challenges for me and my colleagues in government to confront in the months and years ahead. We mean to build on the foundations we are laying at present, and to develop a criminal justice system that is more efficient, better balanced, and more transparent.

CHAPTER 3

Justice for all in the 21st century: the political context of the policy focus on victims

By Sandra Walklate

Professor of Sociology, Manchester Metropolitan University

I am not disposed to take an optimistic view of human life. The hopes of most young people come to nothing. The disappointments of the middle years of life are followed for those who survive them by the ugliness, pain and despair of old age. Most human effort to me is ill directed or dissipated in acts of folly. The pervasive tone of life for most people is boredom, but a boredom made more acute by resentment. (Harre, 1979)[1]

For Harre the key to the avoidance of resentment is respect. This concept is central to the discussion that follows.

Introduction

'Social Being', a book published in 1979, has had, on reflection, a profound influence on my current thinking about victims and victimisation. Having posited the vision of the basic human condition as quoted above; Harre posed few universal laws of human behaviour. However, one of them, of central concern here, is that the deepest human motive is to seek the respect of others. For Harre, the maintenance of respect (and by implication the avoidance of contempt) is

---

1   R. Harre, *Social Being*, (Basil Blackwell, 1979) at p3.

not just an attitude: it is a social relationship. Such a social relationship is predicated upon the premise that human beings have the capacity for self-knowledge, self-monitoring, and self-intervention. In other words they are in possession of what social theorists would call human agency. Put simply, what they do has the capacity to change things. (A capacity developed much later and in a much more subtle way by Anthony Giddens in *The Constitution of Society*.[2]) As Harre goes on to say 'The task of the reconstruction of society can be begun by anyone at any time in any face to face encounter'.[3] So what has all this to do with victims of crime and contemporary criminal justice policy?

1979 and all that: or why are we all victims now?

It is now commonplace to refer to the contemporary social condition in relation to the risk society thesis. Put simply, this thesis posits that we now live in a society preoccupied with the future: the desire to be free from risk. This desire Furedi has referred to as a 'culture of fear'.[4] The processes associated with this preoccupation with safety manifest themselves in diverse ways. Young[5] identifies such processes in the shift from the inclusive to the exclusive society, and Garland identifies such processes in criminal justice policy in the manifestation of what he calls a 'culture of control'.[6] A concern common to these commentators is the rapidly changing social context in which we now all live. In such a rapidly changing context, even the government's own futurologists admit that we are 'leaving behind a social order that we know well and are entering a world the contours of which are dim'.[7] In that context a number of features in relation to crime have come to be taken as common-place.

2   A. Giddens, *The Constitution of Society* (Polity Press, 1984) at p405.
3   R. Harre, above, n1 at p405.
4   F. Furedi, *The Culture of Fear* (Cassell, 1997).
5   J. Young, *The Exclusive Society* (Sage, 1999).
6   D. Garland, 'The Limits of the Sovereign State', *Br J Criminol* 1996 36(4): 445–471.
7   *Foresight*, 2000.

Garland and Sparks[8] list these in the following way.

- High crime rates have become a normal feature of everyday life and avoiding victimisation has become a feature of that daily life.
- The fear of crime has become a highly emotive political reference point.
- There has been an acceptance of a growing private sector and individualised involvement in crime management.
- Crime and the awareness of crime have become institutionalised in the media and popular culture.
- A concern with and for the victim of crime has become not just a symbolic reference point in government policy but a dominant one.

In this kind of social and policy context it is self evident that we live in a society marked by victimisation prevention policy not crime prevention policy[9] put more subtly by Garland as 'responsibilisation'.[10] The processes that these writers are referring to are not necessarily simple nor straightforward but reflect, at a minimum, what Garland[11] has called the criminal justice system's adaptation to failure: an admission that the crime problem cannot be solved, only managed. This is a general portrait of the background against which current criminal justice policy is being formulated. It is, however, worth considering some features of this background in a little more detail, since that will facilitate a better appreciation of why and how the crime victim appears to feature so predominantly.

The changing context of criminal justice policy

Different commentators have highlighted different features of the changing nature of the political and policy context since the end of the Second World War, though there appears to be some common agreement on the heightened nature of these changing processes since 1979. Some features of those changing processes are identified in the table overleaf.

8 D. Garland and R. Sparks, 'Criminology, social theory and the challenge of our times', *Br J Criminol*, 2000 40: 189–204.
9 A. Karmen, *Introduction to Victimology* (Brookes Cole, 1990).
10 D. Garland, 'The Limits of the Sovereign State', *Br J Criminol* 1996 36(4): 445–471.
11 D. Garland, *The Culture of Control* (OUP, 2001).

CRIMINAL JUSTICE POLICY CONTEXT 1950–TO DATE

FROM	TO
Social democracy (Old Labour)	Neo-liberal democracy (New Labour)
'The state': defending and enhancing the public interest	Market prioritised over the state
Parliamentary democracy	Governance not Government
Public services 'neutral': delivering the public good	Public services self interested: not to be trusted.

It is not the intention to debate the intricacies of all of the features highlighted above but to focus primarily on the relevance of two of these features for the discussion here; the shift from Government to governance and the question of the public good.

Government to governance

In order to understand this shift it is important to understand the principles behind policy-making in the post Second World War era. The inception and formation of the welfare state was put in place at a time when government was clearly Government. Put fairly simply the idea of Government alludes to a set of principles sometimes referred to as the 'Westminster model'. This model assumed a strong Cabinet, parliamentary democracy and electoral accountability. However as Rhodes states:

> Since 1945 the institutions of British government have experienced at least two revolutions. The post war Labour government built the welfare state and its institutions, but these barely survived three decades before a reforming Conservative government sought to re-define most and abolish many. Allegedly the Westminster model no longer works.[12]

The revolutions of which Rhodes speaks have been felt in all aspects of the policy-making process including criminal justice policy. One key to understanding the radical nature of these changes is captured by the notion of governance. Rhodes argues that governance is broader than government: 'governance refers to self-organising intra-

12   R. W. Rhodes, *Understanding Governance*, (Open University Press, 1997).

organisational networks'[13] in which the boundaries between the public sector, the private sector, and the voluntary sector are constantly shifting and opaque. Nowhere is this diffusion of influence in the policy-making process more evident than in the context of responses to the victims of crime.

For example, the Criminal Injuries Compensation Board (CICB), now the Criminal Injuries Compensation Authority, established in 1964, was created without reference to the victim of crime per se. In other words there was no empirical evidence to support the establishment of such a body; neither was there a voice speaking for the victim of crime in the policy process. The policy behind the formation of the CICB did have a champion (Elizabeth Fry), but as a policy it was formulated within the principles and framework of the welfare state of the 1950s; that is, informed by a principle of what it was reasonable to expect the state to put in place for its citizens.[14] The same cannot be said today. Not only has Victim Support become one of the most successful voluntary organisations over the last 25 years, now having a central place in informing the policy process in relation to crime victims, but there is also a massive Home Office database in the form of the British Crime Survey that maps the impact of crime and the views of crime victims on a large number of matters. In addition there has been a proliferation of organisations purporting to speak for the victim of crime, albeit not as powerful in their influence as Victim Support but nevertheless vociferous in their claims.[15] In addition, high profile crimes – like the abduction and murder of Sarah Payne in 2000 – have led to particular individuals claiming the ear of ministers. Moreover, it is important to remember that none of the aforementioned groups are elected representatives and none are necessarily accountable to anyone other than their own interests or the interests of their organisations. This articulates very clearly the blurring of the boundaries and the shifting nature of the influences on the policy process conceptualised by Rhodes. There is, however, another layer to these changes.

The existence and proliferation of victims groups demonstrates the continuing 'powerful motif' of the victim[16] and the continued

---

13 See above, n12.

14 See R. Mawby and S. Walklate, *Critical Victimology* (Sage, 1984) for a fuller exposition of this argument.

15 For a fuller analysis of these groups in relation to homicide see P. Rock, *After Homicide: practical and political responses to bereavement* (Clarendon, 1998).

16 A. Bottoms, 'Neglected features of the contemporary penal system' in D. Garland and P. Young (eds), *The Power to Punish* (Heinneman, 1983).

'politicisation of the victim'.[17] However, in the intervening years since the inception of the CICB, the policy-making process has not only become more differentiated and diffuse, it has simultaneously become less partisan and more political. In other words, whose voice is listened to, how, why, when and what about, are all key questions in the current policy climate. This leads to a consideration of the second, though related, theme that it is important to understand in relation to the current political and policy climate: the changing role of public services and what they are expected to deliver.

New managerialism, New Labour and modernisation, or whatever happened to the public good?

New Labour has tasked the criminal justice system with deploying early effective interventions to divert those thought likely to offend from a life of crime: implementing fast-track, efficient procedures from arrest to sentence; improving services to victims and witnesses; enforcing court sentences more effectively; and ensuring the component parts of the system are performing to their maximum potential.

These tasks articulate the current government's vision of how a modern criminal justice system might work where what can be counted is that which works. This is not the place to debate the impact or otherwise of new managerialism or the audit culture on the criminal justice system per se.[18] However, to be found within the impact of these processes on the delivery of public services, in which arguably New Labour has further extended the Thatcherite agenda at least as far as the criminal justice system is concerned, are that notions of the 'public interest' or what constitutes a 'public good' have also changed.

Since 1979 articulations of the 'public interest' have taken a number of forms. Clark et al[19] suggest three representations of this. The first is a view of the public as taxpayers with their interests being

---

17   D. Miers, *Responses to Victimisation* (Professional Books, 1978).

18   See, eg, E. McLaughlin, J. Muncie and G. Hughes, 'The permanent revolution: New Labour, New Public Management and the modernisation of criminal justice', *Criminal Justice* 2001 1(3): 301–318.

19   J. Clark, S. Gewirtz, G. Hughes and J. Humphrey, 'Guarding the public interest? Auditing public services' in J. Clark, S. Gewirtz and E. McLaughlin (eds), *New Managerialism New Welfare?* (Sage, 2000).

equated with economy, efficiency and effectiveness and with a presumed antagonistic relationship with non-tax payers. The second is a view of the public as consumers, as active choice makers within the public services. Hence the various charters of the late 1980s and early 1990s including of course the first Victims Charter in 1990. The last view of the public is one that is still emerging post Macpherson. This view of the public is one of a community of diverse interests.

There are specific difficulties with all of these visions of the public interest. Yet despite the differences between them, they are all surface manifestations of a more fundamental and deeper changing relationship between the citizen and the state. What they share is a common view of the citizen who has rights to call upon the state, but rights that are contingent upon their willingness and ability to fulfil their obligations to the state – a significant shift from the relationship of the 1950s in which the citizen had rights and the state had obligations. In this fundamental shift, managed as it is in contemporary policy terms through modernisation, there is considerable confusion as to what is in the public interest or what counts as a public good.

Waldron argues that a public good is:

> ... something which is said to be valuable for human society without its value being adequately characterisable in terms of its worth to any or all of the members of the society considered one by one.[20]

The value of public goods, then, is not reducible to their aggregate value for each member of society but what they are worth to everyone together. In other words they are irreducibly *social*. Public goods represent something more than their economic worth. Yet what it is that they represent contemporarily seems to be both uncertain and unclear. What is clear and certain, however, in the context of contemporary criminal justice policy, is that sight has been lost of the *social* value of the criminal justice system. Put more generally, there is an absence of a debate concerning what we understand by justice in general, and social justice in particular. In the absence of such a debate concerning the social value of justice, policy makers and politicians can make claims about 'Justice for All' but their ability to deliver is fundamentally compromised since in the 'Third Way' 'what counts is what works' and, for many working within the criminal justice system, what works is that which can be counted! None of which necessarily reflects a *social* understanding of a public good.

---

20 J. Waldron, *Liberal Rights: Collected Papers 1981–91* (Cambridge University Press, 1993) at p358.

Quick fixes and the further politicisation of the victim of crime

Young[21] has commented in more general terms on what he has called the 'cosmetic fallacy' and the 'social as simple' vision of some aspects of criminal justice policy, especially in relation to the various 'zero tolerance' initiatives we have been subjected to. Despite evidence to the contrary the 'quick fix' approach to social problems has become deeply embedded in the contemporary policy process. Nowhere is this more evident than in the proposals in respect of the victim of crime to be found in the government *Justice for All* document.[22] However, from the observations made in this paper on the current influences on the criminal justice policy process, the victim of crime, despite initiatives and protestations to the contrary, is still primarily an imagery being used as a rhetorical political device. Moreover, it is a rhetorical device that seems to be being increasingly deployed to justify the erosion of defendants' rights[23] in the ever-shifting sands of the culture of control. Neither, would it appear, is there a solution to be found in turning to exemplars of European criminal justice policy for our quick fixes. As recent work has shown from France,[24] Germany,[25] and Italy,[26] in those places the notion of the pubic interest and/or the public good has not been subjected to the same processes of 'modernisation' as in England and Wales. Thus, the pessimism with which this paper began appears somewhat justified. There would appear to be little room for manoeuvre to make a real difference to the experience of the criminal justice system for the crime victim. Or is there? What of respect, a notion with which this paper also began.

21   Young (1999), above, n5.

22   Cm 5563.

23   See also B. Williams, Williams, 'Community Justice, Victims and Social Justice', Inaugural Lecture, De Montfort University, 2003.

24   S. Roche, 'Towards a new governance of crime and insecurity in France' in A. Crawford (ed), *Crime and Insecurity. The Governance of Public Safety in Europe*, (Willan Publishing, 2002); A. Crawford, 'The growth of crime prevention in France as contrasted with the English experience: some thoughts on the politics of insecurity' in G. Hughes, E. McLaughlin and J. Muncie (eds), *Crime Prevention and Community Safety* (Sage, 2002).

25   L. Zedner and N. Lacey, 'Community and governance: a cultural comparison' in S. Karstedt and K. D. Bussmann (eds), *Social Dynamics of Crime Control* (Hart Publishing, 2000).

26   D. Melossi and R. Selmini, 'Social Conflict and the Microphysics of Crime' in T. Hope and R. Sparks (eds), *Crime, Risk and Insecurity* (Routledge, 2000).

And what of respect?

There has always been a criminological tradition concerned with the relationship between offending behaviour and the search for respect.[27] So if the maintenance of respect is an important dynamic of offending behaviour, why not similarly in relation to the experience of victimisation? In suggesting this, however, I am not suggesting that we fall into the trap of assuming the need for all victims of crime to embrace a 'victim identity' in order to gain respect. On the contrary, a number of things should be remembered in relation to victims of crime, or indeed the experience of victimisation more generally. Not all victims are nice people. Victims and offenders can be one and the same person. Victims of crime are people trying to deal with more or less exceptional circumstances in their lives. Some of these circumstances they will be responsible for, some of them they share the responsibility for with others, and some things may have 'just happened' to them. How they deal with these circumstances will depend on: their own personal resources (not just economic resources but resources in a more general sense that some social theorists would now refer to as social capital), the resources of those close to them, and the kind of support they may or may not be offered by the various agencies with whom they have contact.

So, if all of that is taken on board, treating people with respect – that is as individuals with personal resources – is key for ensuring that, traumatic circumstances notwithstanding, they are enabled to make use of their resources in order to make sense of what has happened in their lives. A number of implications can be derived from this position. But firstly and importantly, it challenges any presumed 'special' status associated with being a victim of crime. Victims are, after all, complainants in the criminal justice system as offenders are defendants. To use any other terminology prejudges the outcome of a case. Moreover secondly, this position serves to remind us that whilst crime does impact upon people's lives, victims of crime are people too. So by implication, in this regard, it makes little sense to talk of people as victims or offenders, or indeed victims or survivors. They are people and people need to feel OK about themselves and sometimes need some help and support to achieve that. And what makes people feel OK? Respect. Whether male or female, whether a member of an ethnic minority, whether old or young, the maintenance of

27 See for example, P. Bourgois, *In Search of Respect* (Cambridge University Press, 1994); J. Katz, *The Seductions of Crime* (Basic Books, 1988).

respect and the avoidance of contempt sustains a sense of well-being and contributes to people feeling OK. So as Harre said, as was quoted earlier: 'The task of the reconstruction of society can be begun by anyone at any time in any face to face encounter'.[28] So, from this point of view there is ample in place already within the criminal justice system, through various codes of practice and legal opportunity to treat people with respect. What may be required is better education and training to make better use of the frameworks already in place, but more legislation is not necessary.

Conclusion

Victimhood is not a condition to be recommended. Nevertheless, in the face of an increasingly diverse society in which difference is to be not only valued but celebrated, there may still be some value in working with, exploring, and learning from the commonalities of the human condition. Arguably this is especially the case for people who have least resources, either personally or financially, to help themselves. Frequently, all they (and others) want from the criminal justice system is to be treated with respect.

---

28   R. Harre, *Social Being* (Basil Blackwell, 1979) at p405.

CHAPTER 4

Criminal procedure: the rights of the victim, versus the rights of the defendant

By J. R. Spencer QC
Professor of Law, Selwyn College, University of Cambridge

Introduction

I would like to start by posing the question that, in my opinion, ought to be asked at the start of every book on criminal procedure – and which in books on English criminal procedure, regrettably, never is. It is 'What are criminal proceedings for?'

The answer, I suggest, should be the following. Their main aim is the conviction and appropriate punishment of the guilty, and the acquittal of the innocent. Their subsidiary aim, I believe, is a negative one. It is to ensure that, in the carrying out of its main aim, as little pain as possible is caused to everyone concerned. This observation leads on to four matters of perspective.

The first is that the defendant must of necessity be the centre of the proceedings. It is he or she whose behaviour is being investigated, and, if the allegations made against them are found proved, it is he or she who will suffer punishment. Other people's concerns – for example, those of victims and witnesses – are important, and must not be forgotten; but they must inevitably take second place. (In the course of many years of involvement with the law relating to the distressing problem of child abuse, and criminal proceedings relating to them, I have often heard it said that 'prosecutions for child abuse ought to be child-centred'. Alas, this cannot be. When somebody is prosecuted for abusing a child, the child's interests must be taken into account – but there is no way in which the child's interests can, or should, be put ahead of the legitimate interest of the defendant in obtaining a fair trial.)

The second observation is that the main risk we should guard against in criminal proceedings is the wrongful conviction of the innocent – a risk that is more important to avoid than the wrongful acquittal of the guilty. Of course, human beings are fallible, and with them human institutions; there is no way in which the risk of wrongful convictions can be avoided altogether, short of never prosecuting anybody for anything.[1] But we ought to do our very best to minimise it, and where there is a choice of risks, the risk of wrongful convictions is the one that we should choose to avoid. (The situation in civil proceedings is different. When a civil court reaches the wrong result, the miscarriage of justice will not necessarily be worse when the defendant has been wrongly condemned than when the plaintiff has lost the action he ought correctly to have won. But in criminal cases, there can be no doubt which form of miscarriage of justice is the more serious.)

Thirdly, in a civilised society there are (or ought to be) some limits as to how far we are prepared to go in pursuit of criminal procedure's main aim – the conviction of the guilty and the acquittal of the innocent – and the existence of these limits means, unfortunately, that some crimes will, regrettably but inevitably, go unpunished. To take an extreme example: torture. Let us suppose for argument's sake that torture sometimes produces reliable information, and that in certain circumstances the information necessary to convict could only be obtained by using it. Even then, surely no civilised person in the UK today, however authoritarian, would try to argue that the criminal justice system therefore ought to resort to torture. (The debate, of course, is about what the acceptable limits are, and ought to be. Although nobody in the UK would try to make the case for torture today, torture was a routine and official feature of criminal procedure in Scotland until the end of the seventeenth century, and Continental Europe until a century later. Today there is a serious debate about the right of silence – and how far, if at all, it is acceptable to require defendants to give information, and to treat their suspicious refusal to do so as circumstantial evidence of guilt.)

Fourthly, I believe that defence rights ought to be viewed in the light of the main objects of criminal proceedings as I have outlined them above. Questions that it is always legitimate to ask about any right of the defendant are:

1) does it contribute to the court reaching a just result (in terms of the conviction of the guilty and the acquittal of the innocent)?

1   See Glanville Williams, *The proof of guilt* (3rd ed, 1963) p186 onwards.

2) Does it contribute to the conduct of the proceedings in a civilised manner?

If a change in the existing rights of the defence would weaken the position of the defendant, this is not of itself an argument against making it. The proper question, I believe, is whether it would weaken the position of the defendant in any way that undermines the main objectives of criminal proceedings. Would the change lead to more convictions of the guilty, or more convictions of the guilty together with more convictions of the innocent? And would it further, or hinder, the aim of conducting criminal proceedings in a way that causes the minimum pain and suffering for everyone (including the defendant).

As Sir Robin Auld put it in his Report,

> A criminal trial is not a game under which a guilty defendant should be provided with a sporting chance. It is a search for truth in accordance with the twin principles that the prosecution must prove its case and that a defendant is not obliged to inculpate himself, the object being to convict the guilty and acquit the innocent.[2]

To test this, let us consider the right of the defendant to use at trial the weapon of surprise by 'springing' a defence that the prosecution was not expecting. Since the 1960s this right has been gradually eroded by statutory provisions requiring the defence to give advance notice of their intention to call certain types of witness, or if not of the witness, of the general nature of the defence – and further provisions of this sort are contained in the current criminal justice bill.[2A] By eroding the defendant's right to produce surprise witnesses to whose evidence the prosecution may have no time to prepare a challenge, these changes have weakened the position of the defence. However, have they done so in a way that makes it harder for criminal procedure to achieve its proper ends? In principle, the answer surely must be 'no': unless (unlike Sir Robin Auld) we accept the argument that the police are so corrupt that, if they get to know what the defence evidence will be, they will 'nobble' the defendant's witnesses, or suborn false witnesses to contradict them.

To put the matter in a different way, I believe that defence rights should be essentially framed on the hypothesis that the defendant is innocent. They should be framed so as to be helpful to innocent defendants, and not to help guilty defendants get off. Broadly

2   *Review of the Criminal Courts of England and Wales*, by the Right Honourable Lord Justice Auld (October 2001), pp459–460.
2A See now Criminal Justice Act 2003, Part 5.

speaking, a defence right that is helpful to defendants who are guilty should be acceptable only on the basis that its helpfulness to guilty defendants is an unavoidable by-product of a rule which is essential to protect the ones who are innocent. Rules that are particularly favourable to guilty defendants are tolerable only to the very limited extent that they are necessary to serve the secondary purpose of rules of criminal procedure: to ensure the proceedings are conducted in a manner that is civilised, and do not cause damage out of proportion to the object that they seek to achieve.

The traditional position of the victim and the main changes designed to improve it: are they incompatible with the protection of the defendant?

For many years, it was said that the victim was the 'forgotten person' in the criminal justice system. In recent years the position of the victim has been strengthened – but in English criminal procedure the victim is still (at least in theory) poorly placed compared with his or her equivalent in other countries (eg France).

The right to be involved in the decision to institute criminal proceedings

Paragraph 6.7 of the Code for Crown Prosecutors states that

> The Crown Prosecution Service prosecutes cases on behalf of the public at large and not just in the interests of any particular individual. However, when considering the public interest test Crown Prosecutors should always take into account the consequences for the victim of the decision whether or not to prosecute, and any views expressed by the victim or the victim's family.

This gives the victim no legal rights as such, and the victim who does not like the way the Crown Prosecution Service has exercised its discretion to prosecute has only limited room for legal manoeuvre.

In the first place, the victim has the right to attack the decision to prosecute or not to prosecute by using judicial review – and there are several well-known decisions in which victims have used this right successfully.[3] However, 'success' in this context only means that the

3   *R v DPP ex p C* [1995] 1 Cr App R 136; *R v DPP ex p Manning* [2000] 3 WLR 463, [2001] QB 330.

original decision as to prosecution is set aside, and the CPS is required to think again. Thus if the victim persuades the Divisional Court to quash a decision not to prosecute, this does not guarantee that a prosecution will now take place (much less, of course, that the case will be prosecuted with success). Secondly, the victim who is offended by a decision not to prosecute has – like any other citizen – the option of starting a private prosecution. This right, however, is less useful than might at first appear. First, to prosecute a case in the Crown Court the private citizen must in principle employ a barrister, for which purpose there is no legal aid.[4] Secondly, he or she has no legal right to require the police (or any other public agency) to help him or her – by, for example, giving access to their files.[5] Thirdly, if despite these difficulties the victim does decide to start a prosecution, the DPP has a right to take it over and suppress it.[6] Fourthly, the private prosecutor may find his attempt to prosecute attacked as an abuse of process.[7] And finally, if prosecution results in an acquittal the private prosecutor may find himself liable to pay the successful defendant's costs. In a number of respects – in particular as regards the availability of legal aid – the English victim who brings a private prosecution is in a noticeably weaker position than the French victim who exercises his right to start a prosecution as a *partie civile*.

Is there a case for giving the English victim a greater measure of control over the institution of criminal proceedings? Personally I am sceptical.

I do not think there is any case at all for giving the victim who does not want the offender prosecuted a kind of veto. The situation in which a right of veto would commonly be most exercised would be the one in which the wrongdoer was in a position to exercise pressure on the victim – for example, the 'domestic' assault. There are strong and obvious reasons of public policy why, in at least some such cases, the wrongdoer should be prosecuted although the victim now wishes he or she had not gone to the police. In practice, the victim in such cases can already put a significant spanner in the prosecution works by ceasing to co-operate[8] – and that is surely quite enough, if not too much.

---

4   *R v George Maxwell Developments Ltd* (1980) 71 Cr App R 83. In *R v Southwark CC, ex p Tawfick* [1995] Crim LR 658, however, the Divisional Court said that Courts and Legal Services Act 1990 s27(2) had now give the Crown Court the discretion to allow a private prosecutor to appear in person.

5   *R v DPP ex p Hallas* (1988) 87 Cr App R 340.

6   *Raymond v AG* [1982] QB 839.

7   *R v Tower Bridge Stipendiary Magistrate ex p Chaudhry* [1994] QB 340.

8   See *Att-Gen's Ref No 1 of 2003* [2003] Cr App R 29.

Nor do I think there is a much of a case for strengthening the right of a victim to 'go it alone' in a case where the public authorities refuse to prosecute. As it is, the citizen's theoretically unfettered right to bring a private prosecution fits uneasily with the notion of a public agency – the CPS – which operates a structured discretion to prose cute, the detailed contents of which are regulated by an official code. The structured discretion means that prosecutions will normally be brought in certain circumstances, but not in others; and it seems unfair to defendants if, at the whim of a private citizen, they can be prosecuted in a situation where they would normally not be. It was for this reason, indeed, that the Philips Commission,[9] on whose recommendations the CPS was created, wanted the right of private prosecution to be curtailed – and it was only the Conservative Party's enthusiasm for private enterprise in all shapes and forms that resulted in it being retained intact when the Prosecution of Offences Act 1985 was passed. If private prosecutions are sometimes useful as a remedy for official arrogance and inertia, this purpose is now served – perhaps better – by the availability of judicial review.

What about the victim's right or otherwise to be informed about the progress of the case? Paragraph 6.8 of the current Code for Crown Prosecutors also provides:

> It is important that a victim is told about a decision which makes a significant difference to the case in which he or she is involved. Crown Prosecutors should ensure that they follow any agreed procedures.

Once again, this is a provision in the nature of an aspiration, and the question arises as to whether the victim should be given any legally enforceable right to be informed. Giving the victim the legal right to be informed would not damage the legitimate rights of the defendant, in the sense that I interpret them. It might make it harder in some cases for the defence and the prosecution to make cosy deals – but this would obviously not impede the courts in convicting the guilty and acquitting the innocent, nor would it mean that criminal procedure inflicted greater pain and humiliation that is needful to its ends. The practical difficulty is what legal remedy would be available in cases where the victim's legal right to be informed was overlooked or broken. A rule could be introduced that invalidated decisions of which the victim was not properly informed – but the practical consequences in terms of cost and delay would probably be dispropor-

9   Royal Commission on Criminal Procedure, 1981 Cmnd 8092.

tionate to any benefit for victims that resulted. A more promising approach might be to allow the victim, in an extreme case, to attack a decision made behind his back by using judicial review.

The right to be heard: the victim's right to play a part in a public prosecution

Although the English victim has the right to start a private prosecution, unlike the French victim (see above), he or she has no equivalent right to become a party to a public one. This severely limits the victim's right to make sure that the court hears his or her version of events.

In English criminal proceedings it is up to the prosecution and defence to decide what evidence is called, if any. If the prosecution chooses to call the victim as a witness, the victim's story goes before the court. If it does not – as for example where it drops a rape charge in return for the defendant's plea of guilty to some lesser charge, and then sits meekly by while the defence makes a speech in mitigation which blames the victim for leading the defendant on – there is nothing that the victim can do about it. The Criminal Procedure and Investigations Act 1996 contains some complex provisions giving the court the power to ban the media from publishing this sort of 'malicious mitigation'; but, of course, it does not give the person so attacked any right to answer back.

Nor, more generally, does the law give the victim any legally enforceable means of making sure that the court hears the facts that he or she considers to be relevant to sentence – much less any right to convey to the court his or her views on what the sentence ought to be. A step has been taken in this direction by the scheme for what are usually called 'victim impact statements'.[10] However, victim impact statements operate at the level of practice only; they do not give the victim any enforceable right to be heard.

Would it undermine the legitimate interests of the defendant (as explained above) to reinforce the position of the victim to give him a legally enforceable right to answer back when attacked in speeches in mitigation, and to make sure that his version of events is heard by the court when it is called on to decide the sentence?

10 Practice Direction (criminal: consolidated) [2002] 1 WLR 904, para 28, *Personal statements of victims*; A. Sanders, C. Hoyle, R. Morgan and E. Cape, 'Victim impact statements: don't work, can't work' [2001] Crim LR 447; I. Edwards, 'The place of victims' preferences in the sentencing of 'Their' offenders' [2002] Crim LR 689. See also, the papers by A. Sanders and E. Erez in this collection.

I do not think it would. It is obviously beneficial to defendants that English criminal procedure in its current form sometimes ensures that the court is kept in ignorance of the full unpleasantness of what they did – but this does not help the court to sentence guilty persons justly in accordance with the measure of their guilt. There may be sensible objections on grounds of increased cost and delay. But in principle there can be no argument with the proposition that, when imposing sentence, the courts ought to be in possession of all the material facts; and as long as we recognise that the effect of the offence on the victim is a matter that legitimately affects the severity of the sentence, the impact on the victim is one of them.

I think it would also be fair to victims, and not unfairly detrimental to defendants, if victims were given the right to be heard on the matter of compensation orders. As the law stands, a court when sentencing is legally obliged to consider making a compensation order,[11] but the victim has no legal standing in the matter. So if the prosecutor omits to give the court the information that it needs to make an order, or if the court simply omits to make one, there is nothing that the victim can do about it. In law, procedural irregularities are matters for the parties to complain about, and the victim is not a party to the proceedings. If the principle is accepted that it is right for defendants to be ordered as part of their sentence to compensate the victims of their crimes, it is hardly a 'defence right' that the inefficiencies of the legal system sometimes prevent such orders being made.

Protection from publicity

In criminal proceedings, the word 'publicity' potentially covers two very different matters. There is external publicity – meaning publicity to the world in general. And there is internal publicity – meaning the communication of information relevant to the case to the defence.

Whilst some may enjoy seeing their names and pictures in the papers and on television, most people find being publicly identified as the victim of a criminal offence undignified and humiliating. In some cases – for example where victims are vulnerable old people living on their own – broadcasting the fact that they have been successfully victimised can increase the chances of this happening again. Nevertheless, English law does very little to protect the victim from unwanted external publicity.

As regards external publicity pre-trial, complainants in sex cases

11 Powers of Criminal Courts (Sentencing) Act 2000, s130.

are now generally protected. At one time, the media could freely publish the identity of victims of sex offences, and often did, complete with photographs where they could get them. The Sexual Offences (Amendment) Act 1976 prohibited the public identification of any person who was allegedly the victim of a rape, and this protection was later extended in favour of victims of sexual offences generally.[12] In addition section 49 of the Children and Young Persons Act 1933 secures the anonymity of minors who are involved in criminal proceedings, whether as victims or defendants. However, unlike the provisions that protect victims of sex offences, this provision only operates from the point at which a prosecution is begun – and hence leaves the media free to reveal the identity of child victims until a suspect has been charged. Provisions in the Youth Justice and Criminal Evidence Act 1999 designed to plug this gap[13] are not popular with the media and so (surprise!) the government has not brought them into force. Meanwhile, the press continue to make hay while the legal sun still shines.[14]

When the case gets to court the complainant's potential protection against external publicity is wider, because at common law the court can protect witnesses by ordering the media not to publish their identity; and if the order was properly made, a breach of it would constitute the offence of contempt of court.[15] The extent of this common law power is uncertain, and judges exercise it very sparingly. Section 46 of the Youth Justice and Criminal Evidence Act 1999 attempts to add to this by giving the court a general power to ban publication of the witness's identity where to do so is likely either to 'improve the quality of evidence given by the witness' or 'the level of co-operation given by the witness to any party to the proceedings in connection with that party's preparation of its case': but as with sections 44 and 45, the government has so far failed to bring this provision into force.

I believe that the law could and should do more than it does to protect witnesses against unwanted external publicity. The Calcutt

---

12 The current provision is Sexual Offences (Amendment) Act 1992, s7 as amended by the Youth Justice and Criminal Evidence Act 1999 (Sch 2, para 6).

13 ss44 and 45.

14 So when a 17-year-old Eton schoolboy was arrested during the anti-capitalist May Day riots in 2001, not only was he named, but his picture was used to identify him more fully: see Goodman Derrick's *Media Law Bulletin* No. 6.

15 Contempt of Court Act 1981, s11: 'In any case where a court (having power to do so) allows a name or other matter to be withheld from the public in proceedings before the court, the court may give such directions prohibiting the publication of that name or matter in connection with the proceedings as appear to the court to be necessary for the purpose for which it was so withheld'.

Committee on the Press and Privacy[16] proposed to give the court the power to prohibit the publication of the names and addresses of alleged victims, or anything else likely to lead to their identification, if the court believed this to be necessary to protect the their mental or physical health, or the security of their person or their home. I argued for this proposal when I was a member of the Calcutt Committee, and I am no less in favour of it now. Is there any serious argument against it?

The media would undoubtedly respond with arguments about free speech: but I do not think that it is open to any rational objection on the ground that it undermines the position of the defence. Of course, there is an imbalance in the system if the defendant's name is plastered all over the newspapers, while the name of the alleged victim is suppressed. But suppressing the name of the victim or alleged victim does not weaken the position of the defendant, except to the extent that it encourages victims to come forward whom the risk of exposure in the media might otherwise have deterred. That said, I think it is utterly indefensible that English law, while supposedly respecting the presumption of innocence, permits the media to publish the name and address of the defendant ahead of the trial at which he or she may well be acquitted. But this is a wrong that needs to be put right on its own account. It in no way solves the publicity problem for innocent defendants that complainants are made to suffer by the system too.

As regards victims and internal publicity, English law has usually taken the line that the right of a witness to privacy must give way to the defendant's right to defend him- or herself – which means that the defence are entitled to know who the witness is. Despite this, the Court of Appeal in one case[17] held that it was proper to keep from the defence the identity of a schoolgirl who was the chance witness to a murder. This could properly be done, they said, provided the judge was satisfied (inter alia) that the witness had real grounds to fear reprisals, that the prosecution had taken steps to investigate her credibility, and her identity could be suppressed without causing undue prejudice to the defence. In my view, there is no case for extending the victim's or witness's protection from internal publicity any further than this case allows. Who and what the witness is may indeed affect his credibility. If the defence cannot probe the credibility of the prosecuting witnesses, this undermines the right of the defence to

16   Cm 1102 (1990).
17   *R v Taylor* [1995] Crim LR 253.

test the prosecution case which is an essential safeguard against the conviction of the innocent.

Special treatment for victims when giving evidence

Traditionally, the victim – however vulnerable – was expected to give evidence under the same conditions as any other witness. No concessions were made to him or her. The victim was expected to come to court to give evidence, live, at the day of trial. When called upon to testify, the victim had no special privileges (let alone a lawyer to assert them). In principle, this used to mean that the witness had to give evidence under the possibly intimidating gaze of the defendant – no matter how brutally he was alleged to have behaved – and be subjected to a cross-examination in which he or she was called a liar, and asked embarrassing questions about his or her private life in the hope of denting his or her credibility.

In the late 1980s and early 1990s a number of special arrangements were made in order to make life easier for child witnesses: notably the possibility of giving evidence through a live video link, and the possible use in evidence of videotaped statements. Part II, Chapter 2 of the Youth Justice and Criminal Evidence Act 1999 (YJCEA 1999) takes this aspect of the protection of witnesses a great deal further. Building on what had already been done for children, it gives the courts the power to order a series of 'special measures' designed to make it easier for a range of vulnerable witnesses to give evidence. These measures are: when giving evidence, screening the witness from the view of the accused; allowing the witness to give evidence by means of live video link; clearing the court when the witness is giving evidence; allowing the court, during the examination of the witness, to dispense with wigs and gowns; allowing a video recording of an earlier interview with the witness to be played in substitution for his or her live evidence in chief; allowing the witness's cross-examination to be held in front of a video camera, ahead of trial, the tape then replacing the live cross-examination; enabling certain types of witness to be examined via an 'intermediary'; and allowing witnesses who suffer from certain kinds of communication problems to give evidence using what are called 'communication aids'. These provisions are available to *witnesses* who are vulnerable, and are not limited to victims – but they are obviously designed with victim witnesses primarily in mind.

These provisions obviously weaken the position of defendants, to the extent prosecutors can now produce evidence against them that they could not previously have used, because the traditional rules about giving evidence posed insuperable difficulties for certain types of witness. But does this mean that the position of the defence has been unfairly undermined? I do not think so. This would indeed be so if these provisions let in evidence of a type that is unacceptably weak, or deprived the defence of the chance to test or challenge it – but this is not the case. The relevant sections of the YJCEA 1999 are drafted so that a key factor for the court in deciding to order a 'special measure' is whether or not the special measure will enhance the *quality* of the evidence that the witness is likely to give – and all the special measures are constructed so as to ensure that the right of the defence to challenge the evidence by cross-examination is preserved. Thus they do not weaken the position of the defence in any way that undermines the broader aims of criminal procedure, as outlined at the beginning of this paper.[18]

But what is surely wholly indefensible is that the 'special measures' provisions of the YJCEA 1999 apply only to vulnerable witnesses, and do not extend to vulnerable defendants. If the interests of justice make it essential to order special measures so that a prosecution witness who is young, or who suffers from some kind of handicap, is able to communicate effectively with the court, they equally require such measures to be available to help a defendant who is similarly disadvantaged. If they are not, our criminal procedure has become dangerously one-sided – a situation that is almost certainly inconsistent with the equality of arms that is part of the defendant's right to a fair trial under Article 6 of the European Convention on Human Rights.

If there is nothing inherently unfair to the defendant in providing special measures to help vulnerable witnesses communicate their evidence to the court, I do not think the same is true of the other method that the YJCEA 1999 adopts to help victims when giving evidence –the provisions in Part II, Chapter 3, which seeks to prohibit the defence in sex cases from asking questions, or from leading evidence, about the alleged victim's sexual history. If read literally, there is no doubt that the effect of these provisions is to prevent the defendant asking certain questions that could have the effect of casting reasonable doubt upon the prosecution case. This does not merely weaken the position of the defendant: it does so in a way that hampers the courts in their basic duty of convicting the guilty and acquitting the innocent. I therefore rejoice at the fact that in the leading case

---

18 In *R (DPP) v Camberwell Youth Court* [2003] 2 Cr App R (16) 257 it was argued, without success, that the part of these provisions concerning young witnesses were contrary to Article 6 of the ECHR.

of *R v A (No 2)*[19] the House of Lords decided that the court's statutory duty under the Human Rights Act 1998 to interpret statutes to conform with the European Convention on Human Rights prevented them from reading section 41 of the YJCEA 1999 literally: so that, contrary to what the words of the section suggested, a defendant accused of rape was entitled to advance his defence by suggesting that the alleged victim was someone with whom he had an on-going sexual relationship at the time.

Conclusion

In theory, the possible objections to greater rights for victims are three. The first is that they would increase the cost of justice, and the second – often related to the first – is that they would make the machinery of justice revolve more slowly. The third objection is that they would undermine the defendant's ability to defend him- or herself properly, so increasing the chance of being wrongly convicted. All three of these are serious matters: but the risk of miscarriages of justice is surely the one that ought to worry us the most. The danger, regrettably, is that the legislator forgets this. There is certainly room for improving the legal position of victims, but not at the cost of increasing the risk of convicting people for offences they did not commit.

19 [2001] 1 AC 45.

CHAPTER 5

Playing games and cheating: fairness in the criminal justice system

By Jane Hickman
Solicitor

Fairness in the criminal justice system

Since Labour was elected in 1997 a culture of fairness has been developing in most areas of public life, supported greatly by the Human Rights Act 1998. This encouragement of fairness has borne significant fruit in the way the state interacts with the citizen in education, health, welfare benefits and housing. In private law it has become absolutely central to the way that employment relations are conducted.

But nothing like this has happened in crime. Increasingly the criminal defendant is constructed in public discourse as 'the monstrous other' – a figure to be hated and reviled. A defendant is no longer 'one of us'. The imperative on a modern democratic state to guarantee fairness to citizens has attached solely to the victim of crime. A closure has been effected which prevents the presumption of innocence coming into play when the treatment of the criminal defendant is under discussion.

Crime, in particular serious crime, has been on the increase since the 1970s. The media have brought more information about everything, including crime, to public attention. Governments are more readily held to account at the ballot box where greater information is available, and have responded with increasingly strident rhetoric denouncing all forms of criminal activity. In an atmosphere of moral panic about crime, the need for fairness in criminal cases is not as strong as the electoral imperative to secure convictions. Speaking up for defendants is almost impossible in the current climate. Ensuring 51 real fairness for defendants also costs considerably more than just assuming that the investigators are people of good will who must have got it right. Combining electoral arithmetic with economics makes this a no-brainer for government.

This is also exactly the moment when the public has realised that there are genuine grounds for concern at the way it has been served by the criminal justice system. The Macpherson report into the investigation of the Steven Lawrence murder revealed just how badly the criminal justice system can treat victims, witnesses and their families. Much of that bad treatment has been at the hands of the police and judiciary. There are wrongs here which need to be righted. This is rightly high on the agenda for government today.

But as numerous commentators have noted already, fairness to victims is not a zero sum game. It can be achieved without detracting from the rights of the defendant. The fact that this government wishes us to think otherwise is a profoundly political matter. It may have far more to do with the need to cap expenditure than it has to do with the rights of victims. It also serves to cloak the emergence of a deeply authoritarian society.

A brief history of crime

Until the 1960s, in a more stratified social system, both victims and perpetrators were beneath the concern of policy makers. The first post-war Commissioner of Metropolitan Police, Sir Harold Scott, noted in his memoirs, *Scotland Yard*, a 40 per cent increase in woundings since the end of the war but remarked that the offence 'usually arises from brawls or family quarrels and in most cases the injuries are not serious'.[1]

In the world reflected by Sir Harold the experience of the victim was not of interest. To suffer a crime then was to meet with an accident; it was an event without meaning. The word victim does not even appear in his book. Violence and sexual crimes towards women, children and vulnerable people were ignored or condoned, not least by the police.

Nor were these halcyon times for defendants. Under a blanket of silence a series of injustices occurred which reverberate today, including the cases of Bentley, Hanratty and Ruth Ellis. Police brutality and

---

1   H. Scott, *Scotland Yard* (Penguin, 1953).

malfeasance was commonplace. A substantial proportion of criminal cases involved the fabrication of evidence.

But at heart, crime was not the business of the state as it is now. Civil society was expected to train and control its members. Crime was usually detected by the citizenry and there was no great surprise if the police could not find out who had committed a crime. Least surprised of all were the police, who had developed a number of strategies for securing convictions where evidence was lacking.

The change in the way we think and talk about crime was brilliantly captured by Stuart Hall and others in 1978 in *Policing the Crisis: Mugging the State and Law and Order*.[2] Hall concluded that the authoritarianism permitted by a culture of affluence and the welfare state ended with a profound anti-authoritarian crisis during the 1960s counter culture:

> The June election in 1970 marks the official tip of the pendulum, the passage of positions, the formal appearance on the stage of the 'theatre of politics' of a profound shift in the relations between the contending classes and thus in the balance between consent and coercion in the state.[3]

It was during the period of Edward Heath's Tory government between 1970 and 1974 that crime first became a recurrent and highly sensationalist topic in the press. Over the next 20 years the tensions outlined by Hall and others evolved. The authoritarianism which they had observed did not get a clear run. Modes of policing had emerged by the early 1970s which involved the significant application of physical force both on the street and in police stations. The brutality of the police and their willingness to fabricate evidence was all-pervading.

As Hall was keen to note, authoritarianism did generate resistance. From the early 1970s to the mid 1980s a massive struggle was conducted by lawyers, journalists and politicians to establish elementary notions of fairness in the culture of the criminal justice system. Criminal defence lawyers fought a long series of cases in which police malpractice was exposed to the light. Gradually the culture of deference was eroded and juries began to acquit defendants who claimed that police had lied. Popular culture reflected these developments with long running TV serials in which the defence lawyers were the good guys.

2   Hall et al, *Policing the Crisis: Mugging, the State and Law and Order* (Macmillan, 1978).
3   ibid.

A series of miscarriages of justice was uncovered. The pallid faces which emerged into the Strand every month or so convinced a wavering public that something had gone very wrong with the criminal justice system.

At the same time, the problem of police misconduct was highlighted in the most vivid way possible by urban riots. The 1981 Brixton riot led to a public enquiry chaired by Lord Scarman. His report pinned ultimate responsibility for the disorder on aggressive policing methods that had sparked off a wave of violent resentment. His findings shocked many out of their complacence in the same way that the Macpherson Report did a generation later.

None of this was what the public wanted. Reform was inevitable. The Thatcher government yielded to realism and oversaw the most profound changes ever to criminal law and procedure. The 1980s saw the Police and Criminal Evidence Act 1984, the introduction of the Police Complaints Authority, police station visitors and the tape recording of interviews, all of which fundamentally changed the face of policing.

Many have identified the case of *R v Ward*[4] as the high water mark for justice, when the Court of Appeal clarified the sweeping duty on the Crown to make full disclosure of all relevant material gathered in the course of its investigation. At this stage, it appeared that the public had absorbed the lessons of all the miscarriages of justice and that substantial popular support existed for ensuring that the criminal justice system did not make such mistakes again.

To this point, very little had been said or heard about victims of crime. Only singular crimes of the most unpleasant or shocking nature attracted media attention. But gradually attention was turning towards the victim. The killing of toddler Jamie Bulger by two children in Liverpool in February 1993, highlighted by video footage of the child being led to his death by two 10-year-olds, caused great public distress. This happened early in John Major's second term of office, by which time the weakness of his government was already apparent. The Tories seized on the issue to recreate the moral panic of the early 1970s.

John Major used the Bulger killing to launch his 'crusade on crime' in the *Mail on Sunday*. He also reshuffled his cabinet to replace the genial and low profile Home Secretary Kenneth Clarke with hardline right-winger Michael Howard. At the Tory conference in October

---

4   *R v Ward* (1993) 96 Cr App R 1.

1993 Michael Howard unveiled the most Draconian law and order program since the war. There were 27 measures involved, including an end to the right of silence, tagging, limitations on bail and reduction of the right to trial by jury.

Howard took the politicisation of crime to a new level. There followed a series of Acts which laid further burdens on the defendant in the areas of disclosure, severely curtailed right to silence, made sentencing harsher and removed jury challenge.

Labour's dilemmas

While Howard searched for ways to tip the scales further against defendants, Tony Blair was working out what seemed to be a more complex and sensitive position on criminal justice policy. His slogan 'tough on crime, tough on the causes of crime' appeared to offer the public a properly balanced approach to crime, and helped win the 1997 election.

It was some time before civil libertarians realised that it was perhaps only a slogan. The reasons for this were varied. Probably the most compelling was that crime itself had been changing. Not only had it increased in frequency but much of it was better planned, resourced and carried out. These developments were driven by economic factors including the huge increase of public and private affluence and by technological improvements to air travel, cars, computers, and mobile phones.

Where crime has international dimensions it is difficult to find ways of addressing it other than by exclusion and coercion. Being tough on its causes is not an easy feat (as shown by the expansion of the Afghan heroin trade following the defeat of the Taliban). These difficulties are real. However, being tough on the causes of crime in any context is expensive. Being tough on the causes of indigenous crime required a strategy more long term and more financially generous than this government has found the political will to implement.

Yet Labour had made a pitch to the electorate based on doing something about crime that Michael Howard had not yet thought of. Over the last six years Labour's policy in the field of criminal justice has therefore developed considerably. It has sought to apply modern management techniques to improving efficiency. It has managed to demonise not only defendants but also their representatives. It has also made a fetish of appearing to listen and respond to public concern, which may also mean steering a course without any guiding principle. These three approaches have proved a lethal combination, helping to create an ever more effective authoritarian consensus.

Managing by targets

Among the plethora of business plans and targets which have emerged from the Home Office, the Justice Gap Project illustrates the ascendancy of measurable targets in criminal justice policy. The pamphlet *Narrowing the Justice Gap*[5] opens:

> The justice gap – the difference between the number of crimes which are recorded and the number which result in their perpetrator being brought to justice – is the key measure of the effectiveness of the criminal justice system and a crucial indicator of success in reducing crime. This is why the Government has set a new target to bring 1.2 million offences to justice by 2005–06.

Here the government has caused itself major problems. Short of tackling any widespread breakdown of law and order, the most important task for government is to manage expectations of the criminal justice system so that it remains effective in the symbolic realm as a guarantor of social order. Setting it up to fail is not a good idea, nor is the creation of perverse incentives for it to misbehave and convict the innocent. These are, of course, precisely the consequences of what the government has done.

The impact of hard targets on all the criminal justice system players is likely to result in perverse behaviours. This project is a fundamental mistake. The course of justice has been perverted so often by police officers precisely because there has been a scorecard mentality on the part of the state. At the same time this report grotesquely neglects the needs and interests of complainants and witnesses. In the mind of a police officer it will not be kindness and concern for witnesses that achieves the measurable objective, but getting the defendant convicted. And the experience of all those using the criminal justice system will be of failure.

---

5   *Narrowing the Justice Gap*, Home Office Framework Document (Home Office Communications Directorate, 2002).

Thrashing defence lawyers

Being tough on crime has involved being tough on criminal lawyers as well as on criminals.

As the struggle intensified through the 1970s and 1980s to uncover wrongdoing in the criminal justice system, the status of the defence lawyer – and their numbers – increased. For perhaps 15 years, defence lawyers occupied the moral high ground. This was reflected both in their influence in the courts, and the prevalence of several long running TV series in which the lawyer – as investigator and combatant – was hero.

But this position was to change under Labour. The defence lawyer has now ceased to be a warrior for justice and has undergone a process of deconstruction in which his or her economic motives have been laid bare. Unmasked, defence lawyers have been revealed as the greedy, self-serving, fee-generating mouthpieces of the criminal classes. They are the only participants in the criminal justice system who are clearly understood to have an economic interest in it, despite the enormous wealth of many judges and prosecuting barristers, and the dedicated career-building behaviour of many crown prosecutors and police.

There was an initial attempt to integrate the role of the defence lawyers properly as a part of the criminal justice system, but it has been hesitant and readily reversed. The Criminal Defence Service is now charged with making the criminal justice system work smoothly, an arrangement which it appears is not reflected in a wish to hear from defence lawyers in an array of consultative forums. The one-sided nature of policy making is now a significant problem in its own right.

No one seems to think that a defence lawyer will have anything of use to say in the great debate that is now under way. The rights of the defendant are, a priori, already met (or as Paul Clark MP said at the first of this series of LAG seminars, 'everything has been done for defendants'). Given the nature of the political project in hand, it is inevitable that politicians should want to insulate themselves from defence lawyers. Marshalling their own determination is hard enough. An alternative point of view would be messy and confusing.

Most of the policy forums, consultative and working groups in the criminal justice system therefore now exclude anyone who represents defendants – one half of the litigants in an adversarial system. When defence lawyers are present it is in tiny numbers and they are often treated with open contempt.

The exclusion of the defence perspective is part of a larger project which is under way to shift the culture of the criminal justice system away from the human rights preoccupation with fair trial (which is neutral between the parties) to a predominance of fairness for just one party, the victim, (who will become the only party truly to enjoy the presumption of innocence).

Listening to the public

Without a real debate on criminal justice, policy is driven by the need to respond to constituency pressure and to the media. A government that prides itself on evidence based policy-making now runs criminal justice on the basis of anecdote.

Because policy-makers do not listen to defence lawyers, no account is taken of the role and experience of the defendant within the criminal justice system. NACRO cannot speak of the choices that face a prisoner sitting in the cells below the Crown Court, nor can any of the prisoner organisations. The anecdotal evidence is therefore incomplete.

Consequently some of this government's policy-making is driven by something closer to urban myth. For example, there is a persistent strand of belief that defendants benefit from delay. Defence lawyers simply do not recognise this as a discrete or salient motivation for defendants. It was a factor perhaps 15 years ago but is not relevant today. It continues to be said – and believed – by policy-makers that adjournments are caused by defence applications. The only detailed research, commissioned by the Home Office and published in 1997,[5A] was frustratingly unspecific but at least showed broad equality between defence and prosecution in requesting adjournments, with a slight preponderance of responsibility laid at the Crown's door when the non-service of advance disclosure was taken into account. This, however, is not allowed to interfere with policy making, with legal aid rates now set to offer greater rewards to defence lawyers who complete cases with fewer hearings.

A traditional criticism associated with anecdotal policy making is that it lacks rigour and may address the wrong issues. However, anecdote does well in an environment that actually *needs* to side-step a wealth of reasoned analyses showing that the criminal justice system

---

5A C. Whittaker and A. Mackie, *Managing courts effectively: the reasons for adjournments in magistrates' courts* (Home Office Research Study 168, 1997).

has relatively little impact on crime. Criminological study reveals that the reasons why most people obey the law have little to do with the machinery of coercion. What the criminal justice system can do well is to maintain a symbolic order and provide a machinery for dealing sensibly with those who are caught.

The constant resort to anecdote obscures the proper interests of victims. It would help victims a great deal to analyse how all the professional participants in the criminal justice system have tended to turn the system to their own ends. We need to understand why magistrates have been so rude to people, why police do not get back to victims, why the CPS so often takes the easy way out, and why the listing of cases is such a shambolic nightmare.

The absence of analysis and discussion of these issues is not accidental. Police, prosecutors and judiciary have joined together in deploying anecdote so as to control the terms of the debate. Their exclusion of the defence perspective makes scapegoating the defendant an easy way to avoid a more penetrating look at why so many people find the criminal justice system unsatisfactory. The exclusive focus on the defendant and his or her lawyer stands in the way of a real change of attitude within the criminal justice system.

Criminal justice bill

Such a lethal combination of approaches meant that the Labour government of 1997 soon moved to a position more authoritarian even than that of Michael Howard. By 2003 Tony Blair was addressing the Labour Party Conference with these words:

> . . . and of course the criminal justice system with its rules and procedures was a vital step of progress when poor people were without representation unjustly convicted by corners cut. But today in Britain in the 21st century *it is not the innocent being convicted*. It's too many of the guilty going free. Too many victims of crime and always the poorest who are on the front line.

His statement formed part of a campaign of support for a criminal justice bill which has abolished many rules of evidence that evolved over the last 100 years to prevent injustice. This campaign was waged on all fronts, and few holds were barred. Suggesting that a defendant in a criminal trial does not need such protection just because he has a lawyer is an extraordinary sleight of hand. But more sinister is the subtext. Blair knows perfectly well that the the innocent are convicted in the 21st century. Given the statistics of the late 20th century there is no evidence whatsoever to suggest that wrongful convictions have abated. For the prime minister of a government committed to evidence based policy-making this is an extraordinary statement.

The logic of dismantling protection – deregulating the criminal law – is perhaps best summed up in the sound bite from Lord Justice Auld's Report, 'A criminal trial is not a game under which a guilty defendant should be provided with a sporting chance'.[6] This sentiment is ironic given the scorecard approach to criminal justice that is being encouraged throughout the system by projects such as *Narrowing the Gap*. The enthusiasm with which Auld's sound bite has been taken up and repeated by police officers and government spokespeople reveals a deep ambivalence about the game which is being played.

You cannot deprive the guilty defendant of a sporting chance without doing so for the innocent defendant. For those who believe that the acquittal of the guilty person is the greatest miscarriage of justice, this is a reasonable stance. It has chilling implications for those who think otherwise.

'Game playing' started out as metaphor for a fundamental human behaviour, the response of intelligent beings to the existence of rules. It occurs everywhere people interact, whether it is the super rich with tax legislation, in parliament, or in a class of 7-year-olds. Confronted with this reality the only decent, mature, rational and honest response a politician could give is to acknowledge frankly that parties and their lawyers will (and should) always seek to use any set of rules to their best advantage and that the proper response is to provide a fair framework and adequate resources to both sides.

But since Howard launched his anti-crime initiative in 1993 no leading politician has dared to say such a thing. Meanwhile, the long history of police and prosecutors seeking to manipulate the rules has slipped from memory. The current political context does not allow proper scrutiny of all the provisions that undermine the clarity, simplicity and inherent fairness of an adversarial system. Nor does it permit their impact to be construed in the real world of courts and in police stations, staffed by fallible human beings who will at times resort to cheating.

6   *A Review of the Criminal Courts of England and Wales* by the Right Honourable Lord Justice Auld (October 2001), p459.

Prosecutorial cheating

For in truth, the problem is not game playing, but cheating. An adversarial system shares the characteristics of a market. It should be self regulating, which is to say that the chance of a correct result is maximised by allowing the parties to dispute the issue. But the adversarial trial system has the same problem that markets have; that the abstract ideal needs careful regulation in practice because inequalities of information and cheating are universal problems. These problems are to be found in all rulebound human systems, again whether markets, legal systems, schools, etc. This does not mean they are not the best systems, but simply that proper controls are needed.

Markets have been sensibly fettered with rules against cheating, as are educational establishments. Some of the best legislation we have seen in the criminal justice system was expressly designed to deal with cheating – for example, the Police and Criminal Evidence Act 1984 (PACE) – which emerged from the Royal Commission on Criminal Procedure set up in 1978 in the wake of the *Confait* case (where three youths made entirely false confessions to a murder under police pressure).[7]

PACE has transformed policing from the brutal and dishonest affair that it was twenty years ago into a far more sophisticated and successful business, one which commands far greater public consent and trust. But the cheating has not stopped. It has merely been displaced from verbal admissions into other forms of cheating, such as the use of cell confession evidence (*R v Hickey and others*,[8] *R v Stone*[9]), unreliable forensic experts (*R v Clarke*,[10] *R v Cannings*,[11] *R v Dallagher*[12]), non-disclosure (*R v Dudley*,[13] *R v Higgins*,[14] *R v Brannan & Murphy*[15]) and inducements to lay witnesses (*R v Lawson and Williams-Rigby*[16]).

In the light of these cases it is vital that we keep striving to design

---

7   *Report of the Royal Commission on Criminal Procedure* (HMSO, 1981).

8   CCA 30/7/97 (unreported).

9   [2001] EWCA Crim 297, [2001] Crim LR 465.

10   [2003] EWCA Crim 100.

11   [2004] EWCA Crim 1, [2004] 1 All ER 725.

12   [2002] EWCA Crim 1903, [2003] 9 Cr App R 12.

13   [2002] EWCA Crim 336.

14   [2003] All ER (D) 110 (Oct).

15   [2002] EWCA Crim 120.

16   [2003] EWCA Crim 693.

systems that minimise the chances of corruption to the process. Yet the criminal justice bill is a bonfire of the controls that stop the state from cheating.

A fair system

The sophistication of the present government is enormous. It is clearly aiming towards major cultural change in the criminal justice system. It continues to pass laws and change procedures with the primary aim of *signalling* its adoption of a hostile and implacable stance towards the accused (eg the little used 'three strikes' provision, and the widely condemned ASBOs[17]). This is a political project. The real effect of these changes is to make the criminal justice system more expensive and unwieldy. It does not make it feel any better for participants.

The criminal justice system is already experienced as unduly harsh and unfair by defendants. This does matter rather a lot. A vast number of people appear in front of it each year. The experience of fair treatment is vital if its legitimacy is to be sustained. We have been down the road of failing legitimacy in the past. A host of the present reforms are going to make this worse. There is little doubt that the criminal justice system has to change further, but what is dangerous is to let it do so without any guiding principles. For this reason it is worth considering what ideas should guide further reform.

The philosopher John Rawls[18] suggests that trustworthy principles of justice emerge when they are agreed to in an initial situation that is fair. For Rawls the ideal initial situation must 'nullify the effects of specific contingencies which put men at odds and tempt them to exploit social and natural circumstances to their own advantage'. The key characteristic of this primary condition is the existence of this 'veil of ignorance' the provision that they do not know their physical, psychological and cultural characteristics' at the time when the system is established'.

Empirical research in the early 1970s by two American academics, Thibaut and Walker,[19] looked at how a selected group would design the ideal legal system if they did not know what their position would

---

17 Anti-Social Behaviour Orders under the Crime and Disorder Act 1998 s1.
18 J. Rawls, *A Theory of Justice* (Belknap Press of Harvard University Press, 1971).
19 J. Thibaut and L. Walker, *Procedural Justice: A Psychological Analysis* (Erlbaum, 1975).

be in relation to it at time of trial. They found that across Western cultures their research subjects all preferred the adversarial system, sought rules that protected the disadvantaged (ie not the state), and lent maximum control to the disputants.

We live in dangerous times. Some of the crimes with which society must find a way of dealing are truly horrific. These have provided the context for an unparalleled expansion of state powers over the last ten years. We are consequently facing not only the erosion of individual rights but the most authoritarian ideology of the last 100 years.

However, the present emphasis on taking protections away from the defence can be done only on the assumption that we, the law-making majority, will never find ourselves as defendants. That is absolute folly. Miscarriages of justice happen to 'people like us' all the time, or to sons, brothers or neighbours. We need to choose a justice system in which we would be happy to stand trial.

Losing confidence in the ideals of justice and fairness is likely to be the most disastrous of all the consequences which worsening crime brings about. Unless we can realise the ideal of a justice system that treats the defendant fairly no matter what accusation he or she faces, it is less a game than a mere lottery.

CHAPTER 6

Putting victims at the heart of criminal justice: the gap between rhetoric and reality

By John Jackson
Professor of Public Law, Institute of Criminology and Criminal Justice, Queen's University, Belfast

Introduction

In its white paper, *Justice for All*, published last year, the Labour Government committed itself to a programme of radical reform in an attempt to address the various strands of its crime and justice policy.[1] The three strands of policy that were most clearly addressed in the paper were the need for effectiveness in the detection, conviction and punishment of criminals, the need to modernise the criminal justice system and the need to re-balance the system in favour of the victims of crime. The third strand was given considerable emphasis with the government claiming to put victims and witnesses at the 'heart' of the criminal justice system to ensure they see justice done 'more often and more quickly'.[2]

The specific proposals for victims can be broadly categorised as falling into 'outcome-related' measures designed to bring confidence to victims by improving justice outcomes for them and 'process-related' measures designed to improve victims' actual experiences

---

1 See *Justice for All*, Cm 5563 (Home Office, 2002). For commentary see J. Jackson, 'Justice for All: putting victims at the heart of criminal justice?' *Journal of Law and Society* 2003 30: 309. This paper is based substantially on the critique developed in this article.
2 Cm 5563, para O.22

when they come into contact with the criminal justice system. The former feed more directly into the first two strands of Labour's policy in that they are designed to restore confidence by measures which are targeted at offenders who too often escape justice. They embrace the re-balancing strategy referred to above and are to be seen most evidently in the criminal justice bill where a number of measures have swung the pendulum quite decisively in a number of respects against defendants. By contrast, the process-related measures which impact much more directly upon victims and witnesses have been given less teeth and are much more piecemeal in offering help to particular kinds of witnesses rather than witnesses as a whole. It is argued in this paper that this strategy belies the government's claim to put victims at the heart of the system and to deliver 'justice for all' – victims, defendants and the community. The preoccupation with re-balance instead risks injustice to defendants with little tangible benefit in terms of rights and remedies for victims and the community.

The outcome-related measures

The measures designed to improve outcomes for victims have focused mainly on ensuring that those charged with criminal offences are properly convicted and sentenced rather than on the real 'justice gap' which is that so many recorded crimes go undetected in the first place.[3] The assumption that is made is that there is need to re-balance procedures after charge against defendants. Much has been written about the dangers of using 'balancing' analogies in making criminal justice proposals.[4] The idea has often proceeded on the basis of a number of false assumptions. First of all, there is the assumption that a 'zero sum game' needs to be played whereby advancing the rights of defendants can lead only to losses for victims and, conversely, diminishing the rights and interests of the defence will automatically enure to the benefit of the prosecution.[5] This assumption has motivated some of the most fundamental reforms in recent years such as the erosion of the right of silence despite evidence before the changes that

---

3   According to crime statistics referred to in the white paper the police only detect 2.3 per cent of recorded crime: see J. Simmons et al, *Crime in England and Wales 2001/2002* (HOSB 07/02, Home Office, July 2002).

4   See, for example, A. Ashworth, *The Criminal Process; an evaluative study* (OUP, 2nd ed, 1998) at pp30–32; J. Jackson, 'Getting Criminal Justice out of Balance' in S. Livingstone and J. Morison (eds), *Law, Society and Change* (Ashgate, 1990), p114.

5   D. Garland, *The Culture of Control* (OUP, 2001), p11.

diminishing an accused's right of silence would be unlikely to have much, if any, effect upon convicting offenders.[6] Although the Home Secretary gave assurances when he was introducing the criminal justice bill that it was not the government's intention to enter into a zero sum game,[7] many of the critical changes proposed appear to diminish the rights of defendants while leaving question marks over the extent to which they will improve the rights of victims.

A number of examples can be taken. With legislation already in place which diminishes the right of silence,[8] the government proposes to increase disclosure obligations on the defence by requiring a much more detailed defence statement and, going beyond the Auld recommendations, to oblige the defence to give the court and prosecution the names, address and date of birth of each proposed witness. Adverse inferences will be able to be drawn from a failure to comply with these requirements.[9] Civil liberties organisations have raised concerns about the effect these proposals will have on the presumption of innocence and the right of silence and also on the risk that defence witnesses may be intimidated into not coming forward as a result of police contact.[10] Despite an absence of evidence that defence ambushes are actually impeding prosecutions, the intention seems to be to create a level playing field to ensure that both prosecution and defence set out their cases in advance. But even as a balancing exercise the proposal appears flawed. The defence will be penalised by having adverse inferences drawn from an incomplete defence statement. The prosecution by contrast does not have to submit a case statement at all (except in fraud cases). The government would do better to concentrate on more effective means of ensuring that full prosecution disclosure is made, an omission which continues to cause miscarriages of justice for the defence.[11]

---

6 See R. Leng, *The Right to Silence in Police Interrogation: a study of some of the issues underlying the debate* (Stationery Office, 1993). For reports on the impact of the legislation in Northern Ireland and England and Wales respectively, see J. Jackson, M. Wolfe and K. Quinn, *Legislating Against Silence: the Northern Ireland Experience* (2000) and T. Bucke, R. Street and D. Brown, *The Right of Silence: the impact of the Criminal Justice and Public Order Act 1994* (2000).

7 *Hansard (HC) Debs.* Vol 395 col. 912 (4 December, 2002).

8 See ss34–38 of the Criminal Justice and Public Order Act 1994.

9 See Criminal Justice Act 2003 Part 5.

10 See, for example, *Liberty's briefing on the Criminal Justice Bill*, November 2002.

11 A recent example is the failure in the Sally Clark case of the Home Office pathologist to share with other doctors medical evidence suggesting that Sally Clark's two baby boys whom she was convicted of murdering died instead from an acute bacterial infection. See *The Independent*, 30 January 2003.

Another measure taken from the Auld Report is to achieve earlier guilty pleas by introducing a clearer tariff of sentence discount for those pleading guilty, backed up by arrangements whereby defendants can seek advance indication of what their sentence will be if they plead guilty. There has been concern that sentence discounts can put pressure on innocent defendants to plead guilty.[12] The benefits for victims and witnesses are that they do not have to come to court to testify and cases may be disposed of more quickly. But at the same time quicker pleas do not necessarily achieve better outcomes for victims. Charge bargaining and sentence discounts can lead to victim anguish when victims feel that the full gravity of an offence has not been brought home to defendants.[13] The effects might be ameliorated if victims were given greater opportunity to tell their story of what has happened but there is no place for this in the process of accepting pleas. The white paper endorsed the policy of allowing victims to provide personal effect statements but pilot studies have shown that these have had little effect on the sentencing outcome.[14]

Even where the proposals directed at undermining defendants' protections may have the effect of improving justice outcomes for victims, they are clearly undesirable where they risk creating miscarriages of justice for defendants. Another assumption made in the white paper was that victims and defendants should be treated in the same manner in order to do justice to both. This equal balancing approach, however, assumes that the risks of injustice are the same for both. Yet while it is undeniably an injustice when victims see offenders in 'their' case go free, it has traditionally been assumed that it is worse when defendants are wrongly convicted. The government's proposals on the law of evidence, however, start from the premise that the rules of evidence should be rewritten to ensure that all relevant evidence is admissible to help reach a just verdict. One example of this approach is to be seen in the proposals for changing the character evidence rules. Following on from changes proposed by Lord Justice Auld and turning its back on the Law Commission's proposal to retain the presumption against admitting a defendant's bad

12 Ashworth, above, n4 at p288.
13 This has been well documented in rape and domestic violence cases where victims are particularly vulnerable: see, for example, J. Harris and S. Grace, *A Question of Evidence? Investigating And Prosecuting Rape in the 1990s* (1999); A. Cretney and G. Davis, 'Prosecuting Domestic Assault: Victims Failing Courts or Courts Failing Victims?' *Howard Journal of Criminal Justice* 1999 36:146.
14 See C. Hoyle, E. Cape, R. Morgan and A. Sanders, *Evaluation of the 'One Stop Shop' and Victim Statement Pilot Projects* (1998).

character,[15] the government proposes to move towards admitting bad character against defendants when such evidence is relevant to the issues in the case.[16] In the interests of equal balance it is proposed, conversely, to tighten up the rules that govern the introduction of bad character evidence against witnesses and adopt a similar approach of admitting bad character evidence only where its relevance is established. This level playing field approach does not, however, do justice to the different position in which defendants and witnesses are placed in the criminal trial. Besides the humiliating ordeal of having their past character revealed to the court which they share in common with witnesses, defendants of course risk the prejudice that may result from such evidence playing a part in their conviction. It may be that there is a case for an overhaul of the character evidence rules.[17] But the case for reform should not proceed upon the basis that there has to be an equality of approach adopted between witnesses and defendants.

The same point can be made in relation to the hearsay proposals. Here again an attempt is made following the Auld Review to loosen evidentiary constraints by proposing to remove the rule against hearsay and provide instead that hearsay evidence will be admissible on behalf of both the prosecution and defence on condition that certain safeguards are met. The main effect is to admit hearsay when it comes within certain categories of admissibility and in situations where the court grants leave for it to be admitted on the ground that, despite the difficulties in challenging it, it would not be contrary to the interests of justice to admit it.[18] Although the provisions apply to prosecution and defence in equal measure, they have a particular impact on the defendant's right under Article 6 (3)(d) of the European Convention on Human Rights to examine or have examined the witnesses against him or her. The European Court of Human Rights has insisted in various cases that it is insufficient to ground a conviction on hearsay evidence alone.[19] Although it has fallen short of saying

15 See Law Commission, *Evidence of Bad Character in Criminal Proceedings* (2001), Law Com No 273, Cm 5257.

16 See Criminal Justice Act 2003 Part 11, chapter 1.

17 See M. Redmayne, 'The Relevance of Bad Character' *Camb. L.J.* 2002 61: 684 at 700.

18 Clause 98 of the Criminal Justice Bill 2002. This was subsequently amended so that the court will have to be positively satisfied that it is in the interests of justice to admit it. See Criminal Justice Act 2003 s114(1)(d).

19 See, for example, *Kostovski v Netherlands* (1990) 12 EHRR 434; *Unterpertinger v Austria* (19991) 13 EHRR 175; *Delta v France* (1993) 16 EHRR 574; *Saidi v France* (1993) 17 EHRR 251.

that a conviction can *never* be based on hearsay evidence alone, this principle suggests that at the least there should be sufficient guarantees of trustworthiness before this can happen. The criminal justice bill provides that a judge may stop a case if it turns out that the case against the accused is based on hearsay evidence that is so uncon‑ vincing that it would be not be safe to convict upon it.[20] This suggests a fairly low threshold of judicial control. Again the argument is not that there may not be good grounds for admitting hearsay evidence in criminal trials. But changes in this direction have to proceed upon the basis that compensating measures are taken to protect accused persons when they are unable to test the evidence for themselves and it is doubtful whether consigning the entire issue to one of judicial discretion gives the accused enough satisfaction.

Since the issues at stake for victims and witnesses, on the one hand, and defendants, on the other, are of a different order, it is misguided to approach these issues on the basis that each should be given equality of treatment in the criminal justice system. In serious criminal cases defendants face an immediate threat to their liberty which justifies a presumption of innocence in their favour and weighting any errors that may occur in the outcome of the trial towards a wrongful acquittal rather than in favour of a wrongful conviction. If victims are not entitled to the same degree of protection as defendants in terms of the outcome of cases, it is increasingly recognised that they are entitled to protection in the way in which they are treated throughout the process of cases. The European Court of Human Rights has come to recognise, for example, that within the context of a fair trial for defendants, the rights of witnesses must be given protection even though Article 6 of the European Convention on Human Rights does not explicitly require the interests of witnesses and victims in general to be taken into consideration.[21] English courts are also increasingly recognising that there is an important victim and witness perspective to be borne in mind throughout the criminal process.[22] We next must examine exactly how the government proposes to advance the process rights of victims and witnesses.

---

20 Clause 109 of the Criminal Justice Bill 2002. See now Criminal Justice Act 2003 s125.

21 (1996) 22 EHRR 330.

22 See, for example, *R v Brown (Milton Anthony)* [1998] 2 Cr App R 364 at 391, *R v T; R v H* [2002] 1 All ER 683, para 38.

The process-related measures

It has for some time been recognised that victims and witnesses are entitled to rights of services throughout the criminal process such as the need for support and help in the aftermath of the offence and information about the progress of their case.[23] Yet despite over 20 years of initiatives for victims, in a recent review of victims' services, Professor Shapland has argued that states are still not providing victims with very basic and uncontroversial services with the result that victims are still left out in the cold.[24] For example, the 'One-Stop Shop' initiative was designed to provide information to victims of serious offences, yet the pilot exercise found that only three quarters of victims of serious crime were informed about the scheme by the police and of those who opted in significant proportions were not provided with information about their case.[25] The consequence is that despite recent initiatives such as this, victim satisfaction with the performance of the police has declined rather improved in recent years, with only 57 per cent of victims reporting that they were very or fairly satisfied with the performance of the police in the 2000 British Crime Survey compared to 68 per cent saying they were satisfied in 1984.[26]

Recent steps have been taken to improve funding for Victim Support and other groups such as the Rape Crisis Federation and the self-help group Support after Murder and Manslaughter. The Witness Service in the Crown Court has been extended to magistrates' courts and there has been a £11 million investment in the Crown Prosecution Service to enable prosecutors to communicate prosecution decisions such as discontinuing the case or altering charges directly to the victim. There is also now a statutory duty on probation boards to consult and notify victims about the release arrangements of offenders who are serving 12 months or more for a sexual or violent crime.[27]

One of the problems with putting obligations on criminal justice agencies, however, is that they are unlikely to be taken seriously unless consequences attach to non-compliance.[28] In the past, attempts to set

23 Ashworth, above, n4 at p34.
24 J. Shapland, 'Bringing Victims in from the Cold: victims' role in criminal justice' in J. Jackson and K. Quinn (eds), *Criminal Justice Reform: Looking to the Future* (2003), p48.
25 Hoyle et al, above, n14.
26 L. Sims and A. Myhill, *Policing and the Public: Findings from the 2000 British Crime Survey* (2001).
27 See s69 of the Criminal Justice and Court Services Act 2000.
28 See Shapland (2003), above, n24.

out what victims can expect from the criminal justice system in documents such as the Victim's Charter have been vaguely worded and deficient on enforceable commitments and rights.[29] The government has proposed a new statutory code of practice as part of a package of measures in a new victims and witnesses bill.[30] Victims who believe that any agency has not fulfilled its obligations set out in the code will have an opportunity to complain to the Parliamentary Ombudsman. In addition there is to be an independent Victims' Commissioner to champion the interests of victims and witnesses by advising on the implementation of the measures for improving victims services and by making recommendations for further change. Although these measures are a significant improvement upon the Victim's Charter, the fact that they must await a further Act of Parliament in a future parliamentary session makes them appear less urgent than the steps proposed in the present criminal justice bill. In addition it would appear that the new Victims' Commissioner will only have advisory powers, with no specific powers to carry out investigations in specific cases and take action.[31]

When we move away from rights to services and consider victims' procedural rights, the government is even less ambitious in its proposals. Much attention has focused in recent years on how victims can be given greater rights of participation in the criminal process.[32] The government introduced victim personal statements in October 2001 to explain the effect of crime on victims. Of more vital importance to victims, arguably, is their right to give evidence in their case as effectively as possible and for it to be fairly assessed both before and at trial.[33] Special measures under the Youth Justice and Criminal Evidence Act 1999 are being implemented to help vulnerable and intimidated witnesses give their evidence. But these provisions have been criticised on two particular grounds. First of all, they do not apply to vulnerable defendant witnesses and thereby risk breaching

29   See A. Sanders and R. Young, *Criminal Justice* (2000, 2nd ed), pp44–45.

30   See domestic violence, crime and victims bill, introduced into the House of Lords on 27 November 2003.

31   See Liberty, above n10. Similar limitations have been placed upon the Northern Ireland Human Rights Commission: see s69 of the Northern Ireland Act 1998.

32   See, for example, A. Sanders, 'Victim Participation in Criminal Justice and Social Exclusion' in C. Hoyle and R. Young (eds), *New Visions of Crime* (2002).

33   The EU Framework Decision, for example, requires legal systems to safeguard the possibility for victims to be heard during proceedings and to supply evidence (Article 5).

Article 6 of the European Convention of Human Rights.[34] Secondly, it has been argued that in merely 'accommodating' vulnerable and intimidated witnesses within the traditional adversarial trial model, the measures do little to ameliorate the problems that this model of trial poses for all manner of victims and witnesses.[35]

It is seldom appreciated just what a wide array of cognitive, social and emotional skills the legal system demands from witnesses. Witnesses are expected to encode, store and retrieve memories, then communicate memories through the spoken word in a 'foreign context'.[36] Two particular difficulties have been singled out in the adversarial setting: first, the need for witnesses to give evidence at trial, often long after the events in question, in a very public setting in the presence of the defendant and his or her supporters; secondly, the ordeal of cross-examination at trial which witnesses who have given evidence have singled out as one reason why they would not give evidence again.[37] Although the recent provisions enable certain eligible witnesses to have their testimony video-taped before trial and thereby avoid the public ordeal of examination and cross-examination in certain circumstances, these circumstances remain very much the exception and not the norm. First, the witness has to come within the eligible category, then it has to be determined which, if any, of the special measures authorising deviation from the norm are available to the particular witness and, finally, the judge has to be satisfied that it would be in the interests of justice for them to be authorised.[38] Witnesses who do not come within the eligible categories are therefore given no relief, while witnesses who do come within them are given little certainty as to whether the special measures will be used or not.[39] The criminal justice bill does make certain proposals to ease the

---

34 D. Birch, 'A Better Deal for Vulnerable Witnesses' [2000] Crim LR 223 at p242.

35 See L. Ellison, *The Adversarial Process and the Vulnerable Witness* (OUP, 2001).

36 K. J. Saywitz, 'Developmental Underpinnings of Children's Testimony' in Westcot, Davies and Bull (eds), *Children's Testimony: A Handbook of Psychological Research and Forensic Practice* (2002), p3.

37 E. Whitehead, *Witness Satisfaction: findings from the Witness Satisfaction Survey 2000* (2001).

38 D. Birch, 'A Better Deal for Vulnerable Witnesses' [2000] Crim LR 223 at 242. Some judges clearly take the view that videotaped evidence or evidence through live link is a second rate alternative to live testimony: see *R (on the application of DPP) v Redbridge Youth Court; R (on the application of L) v Bicester Youth Court* [2001] 4 All ER 411 and commentary in [2001] All ER Rev 201–204. Cf. *Rowland and another v Bock and another* [2002] 4 All ER 370.

39 L. Hoyano, 'Variations on a Theme by Pigot: special measures directions for child witnesses' [2000] Crim LR 250 at p253.

plight of all witnesses to give evidence. First of all, the previous and original statements of witnesses, made at a time when matters are fresh in their memory and including complaints of criminal conduct, are to be made much more widely admissible at trial and there will be a presumption that a witness in criminal proceedings may refresh his or her memory from documents whilst giving evidence.[40] Secondly, the courts are to be given greater powers in serious cases to permit a video recording of an interview with a witness, other than the defendant to be admitted as evidence in chief of the witness provided the recording was made at a time when events were fresh in the witness's memory.[41] These are welcome provisions in that they show a greater willingness to adduce evidence which is likely to be of better quality than that which could be given in court. It is to be noted, however, that great importance is still attached to subjecting witnesses to live cross-examination at trial, although the courts are to be given greater powers to authorise witnesses other than the defendant to give evidence through a live link in certain criminal proceedings rather than insisting that they come to court to give evidence in all cases.[42] Another proposal already mentioned is that the defence will need to obtain leave before evidence of a witness's bad character can be admitted and that leave should only be granted where the evidence is of substantial assistance in understanding the case as a whole or where it meets an enhanced relevance test by being of 'substantial probative value' to a substantial issue in the case.[43]

Although these provisions go some way towards making the ordeal of giving evidence at trial easier for witnesses, there is no sense in the government proposals that there is a need to take a fresh look at the way in which court proceedings are conducted and at the way in which evidence is generated and assessed before trial. In a far-sighted report published almost 14 years ago into the video-recording of child witnesses, the Pigot Committee considered that there were two principles that should govern the taking of evidence from children: first, their involvement in criminal proceedings should be disposed of as rapidly as is consonant with the interest of justice and, secondly, they should give evidence in surroundings and circumstances which

40 Clauses 104 and 123 of the criminal justice bill 2002. See Criminal Justice Act 2003 ss120 and 139.

41 Clauses 121 and 122 of the criminal justice bill 2002. See Criminal Justice Act 2003 ss137 and 138.

42 Clauses 43 and 44 of the criminal justice bill 2002. See Criminal Justice Act 2003 ss51 and 52.

43 Clause 83 of the criminal justice bill 2002. See Criminal Justice Act 2003 s100.

do not intimidate them or over-awe them, with the smallest number of people present.[44] Although this report was concerned exclusively with child witnesses, the same arguably holds good for all witnesses. Yet the assumption continues to be made that the best forum for hearing witness evidence is at a trial and a 'sticking plaster' culture then holds sway whereby exceptions are made to this mode of taking evidence in particular cases.[45]

More attention needs to be paid to obtaining and assessing evidence carefully before trial so that the cases that are sent forward for trial are fully tested and as strong as they can be. This, however, would require much more effort in terms of finding resources and changing professional cultures than the government, for all its concern about witnesses, appears willing to contemplate. A few examples may be given. First of all, it would require that as a matter of course significant witnesses in a case were video-recorded and their evidence thoroughly probed by the police. The police are under a duty to pursue all reasonable lines of inquiry in an investigation, to record evidence in various ways, to retain evidence and to reveal any retained material to the prosecutor, if required.[46] Too often, however, it is still alleged that witnesses are coached in a particular direction and lines of investigation are closed down too early.[47] A formal video-recording of a witness's evidence would encourage a more searching inquiry. Although the criminal justice bill makes provision for the greater admission of video-recordings, there is, however, no real encouragement given to the authorities to make use of these recordings when taking statements from witnesses. It has been suggested that this would require an extension of the kind of procedures that currently apply under PACE to suspects of crime.[48] At trial a summary or transcript of those interviews that were recorded would then become, or form part of, the evidence in chief of the witnesses concerned, whether or not they accepted it as accurate, which would mean that even if they later diverged from it for whatever reason, there would be a full record of what was said on interview by the police.[49]

44 Judge Thomas Pigot QC, *Report of the Advisory Group on Video-Evidence* (1989), para 2.14.

45 A. Hooper, 'The Investigation and Trial of Criminal Offences in the New Century – The Need for a Radical Change' (1999) 21 *Liverpool L.R.* 131 at p136.

46 See the Code of Practice under the Criminal Procedure and Investigations Act 1996.

47 A. Hooper, above, n45 at p137.

48 ibid pp138–140.

49 The Auld Report recommended that consideration be given to this proposal 'in

Secondly, a truly careful assessment of a witness's evidence before trial would require much greater scrutiny by prosecutors who have to make the decision whether to prosecute. Recent pilot studies monitoring the effect of giving prosecutors the decision to charge suggest that this is giving prosecutors a much greater role in the investigation of cases as they are in a position to ask that certain inquiries are made before charge.[50] But this change may not go far enough. One of the concerns raised in the Damilola Taylor case in which two defendants were acquitted of the murder of a black youth on the judge's direction, was that the evidence of a 12-year-old girl who was the only eye-witness to claim to have seen the murder occur had not been properly tested in advance of the trial. A report into the investigation of the case considered that the witness should have been interviewed in better ways and commented on the absence of any process to test her veracity before trial.[51] A review of the case by the DPP highlighted the fact that no prosecutor – whether a CPS reviewing officer or independent counsel – ever speaks to a victim or witness about their evidence before someone is charged.[52] The result is that in many cases which depend on the credibility of a single witness the prosecutor will normally have only the written statement of the victim, a record of the interview with the suspect and perhaps the opinion of the officers who spoke to both of them, upon which to make a judgement whether to prosecute. Ironically, the criminal justice bill puts the final nail in the coffin of committal proceedings which were at least one mechanism, albeit one that was infrequently used, for testing the witness's evidence in advance of trial.[53] The DPP review concluded that any change to the existing position in England and Wales to allow direct access to witnesses would require changes to the professional codes of conduct. This is an indication of the importance of changing professional culture if there is to be any effective testing by prosecutors of prosecution witnesses before trial.

Finally, if cases are to be dispensed with quickly to enable proceedings to be brought to a conclusion within a reasonable time, it would

the long term': see *Review of the Criminal Courts of England and Wales* by the Right Honourable Lord Justice Auld (October 2001), chapter 11, para 94.

50 See P. Goldsmith, 'The Developing Role of the Modern Prosecutor' (2002), The Kalisher Memorial Lecture 2002, p5.

51 *The Review of the Investigation and Prosecution Arising from the Murder of Damilola Taylor* (2002), paras 6.15 and 6.16.

52 See *DPP's Findings in Damilola Taylor Case* (2002), available at www.cps.gov.uk/Home/PressArchives/153-02.htm.

53 See schedule 3 to the Criminal Justice Act 2003.

seem that more needs to be done to tackle the 'adjournment culture' which has been said to be such a prominent feature of the criminal process before trial.[54] Case management was one of the major concerns of the Auld Review and much effort has been expended in recent times in trying to reduce delay, especially in youth cases. A number of measures known as the 'Narey reforms' have been introduced and the government would seem to have met its pledge to halve the time it takes to deal with persistent young offenders from arrest to sentence by half.[55] These managerial initiatives have focused on setting targets which deal with average times taken to deal with cases but they do not guarantee that all cases will be dealt with within a reasonable time. Article 6 of the European Convention on Human Rights requires that everyone charged with a criminal offence is brought to trial within a reasonable time and although this is aimed at defendants, the courts are also recognising the harmful effects that delays can have upon victims of crime.[56] Another approach which is a more effective means of ensuring compliance with human rights standards is to concentrate on actual time limits which apply to all cases and can be backed up with sanctions where appropriate.[57] The Auld Review was against the introduction of overall time limits for cases on the ground that experience in other jurisdictions such as Scotland suggested that rigid or vigorously applied over-all time limits can be counterproductive.[58] But the government has already imposed custody time limits and has piloted overall time limits in youth cases.[59] It may be that this is the way forward for certain kinds of cases where urgency is particularly pressing such as youth cases and others involving vulnerable witnesses and defendants. Such an approach need not be as inflexible as the Auld Report suggested, as there is provision in the legislation for time extensions in cases where delay was not the fault of the

---

54 See, for example, the comments of Chris Mullin MP during the debate in the House of Commons of the Criminal Justice Bill: *Hansard (HC) Debs*, Vol 395 col. 943 (4 December 2002).

55 W. Lowe and J. O'Brien, *Average Time for Arrest to Sentence for Persistent Young Offenders: January – March 2002* (2002).

56 See, for example, *HM Advocate v P*, 2001 SLT 924, *Dyer v Watson and Burrows*, 2002 SC (PC) 89.

57 J. Jackson, J. Johnstone and J. Shapland, 'Delay, Human Rights and the Need for Statutory Time Limits in Youth Cases' [2003] Crim LR 510.

58 Above, n49, chapter 10, para. 263.

59 Provision is made for custody time limits and overall time limits in s22 of the Prosecution of Offences Act 1985 and ss43–45 of the Crime and Disorder Act 1998.

prosecution and even for reinstating cases that have been stayed as a result of a breach of the limits.[60] The youth pilot scheme has been evaluated positively, yet the government appears to have turned its back on this initiative.[61]

Conclusion

Although the government has introduced a number of measures that should result in better treatment and services for victims and witnesses in the course of criminal cases, it is suggested that not enough urgency has been given to what may be regarded as the fundamental right of victims and witnesses to have their evidence properly heard without fear of intimidation and to have their case dealt with as promptly as possible. A policy of permitting special measures for particular kinds of vulnerable and intimidated witnesses has been implemented but this does not tackle the more fundamental question of how matters might be eased for *all* victims and witnesses.

This would require a more searching review of the procedures for taking witnesses' evidence before trial and at trial. Although the vast majority of cases are disposed of without a trial, the adversarial criminal trial continues to be the main testing ground for assessing witnesses' evidence and there has been a failure to conduct comparative analysis of less adversarial jurisdictions where it has been claimed that victims and witnesses fare better.[62] Instead, as we have seen, the government is putting considerable energy in its criminal justice bill into re-balancing the trial in favour of the prosecution against the defence by abolishing or severely diluting many of the traditional safeguards that defendants have enjoyed at trial. The result is to make defendants more vulnerable at trial without seriously advancing the rights of victims and witnesses, as the majority of them will have to

60 See ss43(2) and 45 of the Crime and Disorder Act 1998 amending s22 of the Prosecution of Offences Act 1985.

61 See J. Shapland et al, *Evaluation of Statutory Time Limit Pilot Schemes in the Youth Court – Final Report* (2003), RDS OLR 21/03, available at www.homeoffice.gov.uk/rds/pdfs2/rdsolr2103.pdf.

62 See, for example, W. T. Pizzi and W. Perron, 'Crime Victims in German Courtrooms: A Comparative perspective on American Problems' (1996) 32 *Stanford Journal of International Law* 37 at 41. See also Ellison, above, n33 at p148. It has been suggested, however, that Ellison's actual findings regarding the treatment of rape complainants suggest that they do not fare much better in an inquisitorial setting, see K. Quinn, 'Justice for Vulnerable and Intimidated Witnesses in Adversarial Proceedings?' (2003) 66 *Modern LR* 139 at p152.

endure the same ordeal of examination and cross-examination about events that may have happened some time ago.

All this calls into question the government's aim of delivering 'justice to all'. A true 'justice for all' policy, arguably, needs to take a more explicit rights-centred approach than the government has been willing to take despite its enactment of the Human Rights Act 1998. This would identify what rights witnesses, victims and defendants are entitled to within the general safeguard of a fair trial and approach reform on that basis.[63] Specific remedies would be prescribed for individuals when their rights had been infringed with the result that there would be consequences for criminal justice agencies that failed to deliver these rights. Only when agencies are required to give meaningful consideration to the rights of victims and witnesses will it be able to be claimed that they have been brought in from the cold and put more at the heart of the criminal justice system.

---

63 A. Ashworth, 'Victims' Rights, Defendants; Rights and Criminal Procedure' in A. Crawford and J. Goodey (eds), *Integrating a Victim Perspective within Criminal Justice* (2000), p185.

CHAPTER 7

Integrating restorative justice principles in adversarial proceedings through victim impact statements

By Edna Erez

Department of Justice Studies, Kent State University

The increased interest in restorative justice to address crime and delinquency has proceeded under the presumption that the two systems – restorative and adversarial justice – are distinguished and separate, and cannot, conceptually and practically, co-exist. This article attempts to demonstrate the utility of the victim impact statement (VIS), or victim personal statement (VPS) – its counterpart in the United Kingdom[1] – as a measure that produces the benefits of restorative justice practices in adversarial justice systems, without interfering with adversarial principles or violating defendant rights.

The article first reviews the history of the VIS reform, providing backgound to some of the persisting objections to victim voice in

---

1   The distinction between the VIS and the VPS, as discussed below, resulted from a misreading of the reform purpose and related research. In this article, the term VIS is used as a generic term to denote providing victim impact materials at/for sentencing. It does not address victim statement of opinion (VSO), in which victims provide their opinion about an appropriate sentence. The VSO is practiced only in a small number of jurisdictions, and is not a widely accepted part of the victim rights package. The article does not address the use of VIS in capital cases, which has attracted much of the opposition to the VIS in the United States. Most western countries do not use death sentences as as a penalty option.

sentencing.[2] It then examines recent research that supports the use of VIS to increase victim and offender communication and enhance victim welfare. The article concludes with policy recommendations for legal professionals about the way to maximise the benefits that victim input rights provides to victims, offenders and the adversarial justice system

Background of the VIS reform

The concern over the 'secondary wounds' inflicted on victims in the criminal justice process, particularly the absence of a victim voice in proceedings, led to a victim movement that mobilised to ameliorate the plight of victims. Providing victims input rights was a measure to reduce victim trauma and alienation from the system. The VIS reform allowed victims to describe in open court the harm they sustained, and their remaining concerns or fears related to the victimisation. It was created to address simultaneously victims' 'perceived justice needs,'[3] and promote their psychological welfare. These two issues were viewed as interconnected, if not inseparable.

The idea of victim voice at sentencing has met with fierce resistance by the legal profession, which found the thought of allowing emotional victim input in courtroom unacceptable.[4] Legal professionals and scholars argued that victim input would violate fundamental principles of adversarial legal systems, which do not recognise the victim as a party to the proceedings. Including victim input, it was claimed, would transform the trial between the state and the defendant to tripartite court proceedings, lead to harsher sentences, and introduce an element of inconsistency in sentencing. Particular objections were raised regarding allocution rights for victims, as it was

2   A. Ashworth, 'Restorative Rights and Restorative Justice' *Br J Criminol* 2002 42: 578–595; A. Sanders, C. Hoyle, R. Morgan and E. Cape, 'Victim Impact Statements: don't work, can't work' [2001] Crim LR 447–458. See also I. Edwards, 'Victim Participation in Sentencing: the problems of incoherence' *The Howard Journal*, 2001 40(1): 30–54.

3   L. Sebba, *Third Parties: victims and the criminal justice system*, (Ohio State University Press, 1996).

4   In England, the idea of victim input was described as the 'pollution' of criminal proceedings with emotion: see 'The Role of Victims in the Criminal Justice Process' (1996, Home Office Special Conference Unit). The importance of emotions in the study of crime, law and criminal justice decision-making has been recently revived. See presidential address by Professor Larry Sherman, the President of the American Society of Criminology, delivered at the ASC annual meeting in Chicago, and published in the August 2003 issue of *Criminology*.

feared that victim speech may be moving for the judge or jury, and result in an increase in sentence severity or disparity.[5] Victims were also portrayed as vindictive, punitive, and motivated by a desire to maximise sentence severity. Concern for defendants' rights was a recurrent argument invoked against the use of VIS,[6] postulating that victim input rights were established to benefit the prosecution and therefore harm defendants.[7]

Because the campaign to provide victims with a voice encountered a strong opposition, the justification for the reform was quickly refashioned to emphasise the VIS potential to aid the court in sentencing, rather than a measure to provide victims a voice. The reform was 'sold' to adversarial legal systems primarily as a tool to help judges impose sentences commensurate with the (intended) harm.[8] The presentation of the VIS in adversarial systems as a valuable tool for judges in meting out 'justice' underlies the legal discourse of adversarial legal systems regarding the purpose of the VIS.

The legal discourse about VIS and related research

In line with the revised purpose of the reform as a tool to 'help' the court in sentencing, the discourse regarding the justifications for the VIS reform by and large did not address victims' need for expression. For instance, for the prosecution, the VIS was presented as a tool to provide an exact measure of the harm sustained by the victim, details on the victim's need for reparative sanctions, or the appropriate conditions that might be imposed on the offender. For judges, the

5   Other legal objections included the principle that unforeseen harm should not used to increase sentence severity eg A. Ashworth, 'Victim Impact Statements and Sentencing' [1993] Crim LR, 498–509. Practical concerns included the adverse effects that victim input may have on court resources and scheduling.

6   A. Ashworth, 'Victims' Rights, Defendants rights and Criminal Procedure' in A. Crawford and J. Goodey (eds), *Integrating a Victim Perspective in Criminal Justice: International Debates* (Ashgate, 2000) at pp185–204. See also Edwards (2001), above, n2.

7   See E. Erez, 'Victim Participation in Sentencing: and the debate goes on . . .', *International Review of Victimology*, 1994 3:17–32 for discussion of the arguments against the VIS. The argument about violation of defendant rights may have some face value. However, as will be discussed below, there has been little evidence that violations of defendants' rights have occurred in the VIS context.

8   Edwards (2001), above, n2, describes the multiple rationales used by politicians and members of legislative bodies in the United States, England and South Australia to pass VIS legislation leading to incoherence and contradictory expectations for the reform.

VIS was intended to ascertain that they become aware of the full details of the offence so that they could impose a proportionate sentence. From the court's perspective, the VIS was construed as an opportunity to recognise the wrong committed against an individual victim, promoting the idea that although crimes are committed against the state, it is the individual citizen who suffers loss, damage or injury. The VIS was also offered as benefiting other participants, including offenders' rehabilitation, by helping defendants confront the harm that they have inflicted on the victim.

The emphasis on the instrumental function of the VIS as a tool to inform judges' sentencing decisions has derailed the VIS from its original purpose as a mechanism for victim voice. It redirected debates about the reform to questions such as whether the VIS fulfils its intended usage, meets the needs of the court, or what are the reform's unanticipated results. It also prompted research which focused on these issues, particularly the impact of VIS on sentencing.[9] The expressive purpose of the VIS and its utility as a therapeutic opportunity for victims to convey their ordeal to the court (and in some cases to the offender) have been forgotten, as critics were engaged in debating the reform impact on sentencing.[10]

In light of research findings that the filing of VIS does not increase sentence severity, critics argued that VIS are merely 'sweeteners,' or were created 'to fool victims into believing that they can influence sentencing outcomes'.[11] They maintained that while it may be politically correct to employ the rhetoric of victim input,[12] victims would be better served by having 'substantive' rights, or services, rather than 'procedural'[13] rights, such as the VIS.[14] Victims' welfare, it was claimed, would be improved by offering them explanations about

9   See summary in E. Erez, ' Who Is Afraid of the Big Bad Victim: victim impact statements as victim empowerment and enhancement of justice' [1999] Crim LR 545–556.

10   This preoccupation with the instrumental view of VIS is the major reason for the bold, though misguided, conclusion of Sanders, Hoyle, Morgan and Cape [2001] Crim LR 447–458 that VIS 'don't work, can't work'.

11   See Ashworth (2000), above, n6.

12   eg Edwards (2001), above, n2.

13   The definition of the VIS as a procedural right expressed by English scholars (eg Ashworth, 1993, 2000; Sanders et al, 2001; Edwards, 2001) is another misguided conception of the VIS. For victims, as this discussion show, the VIS fulfills a human need that should be 'serviced' (in the terminology of Ashworth, 1993), rather than constituting a 'procedural' right newly added to victims in adversarial legal systems.

14   Ashworth (2000), above, n6.

the sentencing process and court outcomes, as opposed to input rights.[15]

The preoccupation with VIS impact on sentencing is the unfortunate confluence of prevailing definitions of VIS as a tool to inform judges about victim harm, and the thrust of VIS related research, which evaluated the VIS impact on sentencing outcomes.[16] The focus on instrumental functions of the VIS, particularly its presumed aim to 'influence sentences',[17] has diverted attention from the restorative function of the VIS.

Influencing the sentence, however, has never been an explicit or implicit purpose of the VIS legislation. Historically, and at the present, the primary function of the VIS legislation was expressive – to provide crime victims with a 'voice', regardless of any impact it may have on sentencing.[18]

Evaluation reseach, VIS and victim welfare

Critics claimed that the goal of improving victim welfare, or the therapeutic benefits of having a voice, was merely rhetoric, if not an illusion. Research findings on the topic were interpreted in a way that supported objections to victim input in sentencing. For instance, although the Hoyle et al (1998) evaluation study of the One Stop Shop found that the majority (two thirds) of the victims submitting VIS did so for 'therapeutic' and expressive reasons, they did not consider the VIS important for victim's healing. Instead, they relied on another finding – that over half of the victims submitted the VIS to influence the sentence – to discredit the VIS value for victims' welfare, arguing that victims' desire to impact sentences is the primary motive for submitting a VIS.[19] Although their research found that the majority (77 per cent) of victims stated at the time they submitted the VIS that the act of submission was helpful, and 'only' 59 per cent felt so at the end

---

15 Sanders, Hoyle, Morgan and Cape (2001), above, n2.

16 See summary in E. Erez, ' Who Is Afraid of the Big Bad Victim: victim impact statements as victim empowerment and enhancement of justice' [1999] Crim LR 545–556.

17 Sanders et al (2001), above, n2. See also I. Edwards, 'The place of victims' preferences in the sentencing of "their" offenders', [2002] Crim LR 689.

18 Erez (1999), above, n9 ; J. V. Roberts and E. Erez, 'Communication in sentencing: exploring the expressive function of Victim Impact Statements', *International Review of Victimology*, 2004 10: 223–244.

19 Sanders et al (2001), above, n2.

of the process, the Sanders et al (2001) team concluded was that the VIS is a failure. The small reduction (18 per cent) in the number of victims who were satisfied with the submission of the VIS was considered conclusive evidence for the reform's failure. Similarly, an increase of 15 per cent in victim satisfaction found in the VIS studies conducted in the US does not justify for Sanders et al (2001) integrating victims in sentencing, thereby meddling with sacred adversarial legal routines.[20] They concluded that despite the VIS 'rhetorical and political appeal',[21] victim input has no place in sentencing.

Research and practical experience have shown that, by and large, victims are not interested in changing sentencing outcomes,[22] nor do they want decision-making powers.[23] Whether the avowed aims of the VIS are phrased in terms of benefits to court officials, other trial participants, or the sentencing system as a whole, and whether the VIS purpose is framed within a discourse of rights, enhancing system efficiency, improving services or outcomes, or as restorative justice/ therapeutic jurisprudence elements,[24] promoting victim welfare through expression has been the motive for the reform and the driving force behind the VIS.

Victim voice, satisfaction with justice, and recent victim related research

There is ample evidence that providing input at sentencing is beneficial to the victims.[25] Recent research identified three major factors

---

20 Sanders et al (2001), above, n2.

21 Edwards (2001), above, n2, at p44; see also Sanders et al (2001), above, n2.

22 Victims sometimes state that they want their input to help in 'doing justice' or that their input should be considered in sentencing, but such statements are not evidence that this wish is what motivates victims to provide input. Most studies on the subject show that this interest is secondary as best, see U. Orth, 'Secondary Victimisation of Crime Victims by Criminal Proceedings' *Social Justice Research*, 2002 15(4):313–326.

23 See H. Reeves and K. Mulley 'The New Status of Victims in the UK: opportunities and threats' in A. Crawford and J. Goodey (eds), *Integrating a Victim Perspective in Criminal Justice: international debates* (Ashgate, 2000) at pp125–145. Because Reeves also construes the VIS as having the purpose of influencing the sentence, or to provide victims decision-making powers, in the past she has objected to the reform. Recently Reeves has conceded to allowing the VPS, which she, like others in England, perceive it to differ from the VIS as it is not collected to influence the sentence.

24 eg Edwards (2001), above, n2.

25 This applies mostly to victimisations in violent crimes, particularly serious

that increase victims' overall satisfaction with the justice system and reduce their trauma. They include procedural justice concerns (eg having opportunity to be heard, being treated with respect, being informed and involved in key justice proceedings related to their cases, being taken seriously and being believed[26]), the overall decision of the court (eg whether the victims received financial compensation, information on the offender's intent), and admission of guilt or request for forgiveness from the perpetrator.[27] These factors were found to have more explanatory power than the severity of punishment. This research suggests that victims interests or concerns relative to proceedings, are not tantamount to imposing a severe sentence, but pertain to the court addressing a broad range of issues that are within its purview, issues that a well implemented VIS programme can facilitate.

Recent research which surveyed actual victims about their subjective punishment goals,[28] identified public recognition of victim status as the most significant goal of victims.[29] The study confirmed that victims experience the refusal of victim status as secondary victimisation, and that the VIS can well serve victims by recognising their victim status.The findings suggest that a VIS is not only a procedural right (although from a legal/court perspective the VIS may be viewed as such)[30] but it constitutes a substantive benefit for victims. To them, the VIS is not merely a protocol or procedure to follow but rather a measure that fulfills a need for expression[31] and an important way to recognise their status as victims.[32]

ones, although it may occur in other crimes as well. See J. Wemmers, 'Restorative justice for victims of crime: a victim-oriented approach to restorative justice', *International Review of Victimology*, 2002 9: 43–59.

26 See for instance, J. Wemmers, *Victim in the Criminal Justice System* (Kugler Publications, 1996)

27 U. Orth 'Secondary victimisation of crime victims by criminal proceedings', *Social Justice Research* 2002 15(4): 313–326. See also Wemmers (1996), above n26.

28 U. Orth, 'Punishment Goals of Crime Victims', *Law and Human Behavior*, 2003 27(2): 173–186.

29 The recognition factor was irrelevant or non-existent in studies of punishment goals of the general public. See Orth (2003), above, n28.

30 See Ashworth (1993), above, n5 and (2002), above, n2; Sanders et al (2001) above, n2; Edwards (2002), above, n2.

31 J. W. Pennebaker, *Opening Up: The Healing Power of Confiding in Others* (William Morrow, 1990)

32 Orth (2003), above, n28.

A common criticism of the right for input is the 'dashed expectations' argument.[33] Studies suggest that for some victims, providing them with input rights raises their expectations to influence the sentence, and when they feel that their input had no impact, they become dissatisfied.[34] Several responses are in order. First, victims do not have a baseline of sentence severity with which they can compare the outcome in their case. Victims, like the public in general, tend to view sentences as too lenient. This perception can be altered by providing victims with explanations about the range of sentences in like cases and the factors judges use in determining penalties. Such explanations should be offered to victims prior to their involvement in criminal justice proceedings on a routine basis.[35] Second, VIS forms which instruct victims to fill out a VIS for the purpose of sentencing (as many standard VIS forms do), rather than for communication with the judge and offender, may create or heighten expectations that their input would influence the sentence.[36] Available research on victims' subjective punishment aims would suggest that victims would choose to fill out VIS forms even if they were told that their statement would not affect the sentence. Most victims' input is motivated by the need to express the ordeal and to be recognised as victims.[37] Stating that the VIS is as much addressed to the offender as it is to the judge may also prevent victims' assumptions that the purpose of the VIS is to influence the sentence rather than facilitate exchanges between victims and offenders, as restorative justice would suggest.[38]

33 See A. Ashworth, 'Victim Impact Statements and Sentencing', [1993] Crim LR 498.; Sanders et al (2001) above, n2; Edwards (2002), above, n2.

34 Such dissatisfaction was in fact documented for some victims who submitted a VIS in E. Erez and P. Tontodonato, 'Victim Participation in Justice and Satisfaction with Justice', *Justice Quarterly* 1991 9(3): 393–427. Considering the importance of victim expression for victim welfare, commentators should attempt to study the reasons behind victim disappointment and find constructive ways to prevent it rather than merely repeat this finding or use it as evidence against implementing the reform.

35 Erez (1999), above, n9.

36 Roberts and Erez (2004), above, n18.

37 Orth (2002), above, n26 and (2003), above, n28.

38 There is other information that can help victims understand sentencing outcomes, eg explanation of the various considerations used by judges to determine sentencing outcomes: see Erez (1999), above, n9.

Restorative justice aspects of the VIS

In the last two decades, recognition of the importance of victim voice in proceedings,[39] on one hand, and victims' role in the re-entry of offenders[40], on the other has increased. This transformation is due in part to victim advocates' relentless efforts on behalf of victims, and research findings which challenged prevailing beliefs and myths about victims' motives and interests, and the consequences of providing input into sentencing.[41]

Crime victims, particularly of serious offences, are eager to express their ordeal. They want to communicate their harm, more than they wish to influence the sentence.[42] In this context, the VIS can be construed as a restorative justice element in adversarial proceedings, facilitating court supervised communication between victims and offenders. In contemporary debates, however, the two models of justice, adversarial and restorative, are distinct and mutually exclusive, and victim expression is considered appropriate for one, ie, restorative justice, but not for the other.[43]

The VIS is a remedy that injects restorative justice elements into adversarial proceedings.[44] The National Institute of Justice (NIJ), which is the US Department of Justice research and evaluation arm, describes on its website the VIS as the first item on the examples it provides for restorative justice practices. The VIS is listed in this link together with restorative justice remedies or practices such as restitution, sentencing circles, community service, family group conferencing, victim offender mediation, victim impact panels and victim impact classes. The NIJ website defines the VIS as 'one of the most effective means to communicate the 'voice of the victim' throughout the criminal and juvenile justice systems.' It does not mention at all its function or utility for the court.

39   Erez (1999), above, n9 and Sanders et al (2001), above, n2.
40   S. Herman and C. Wasserman, 'A Role for Victims in Offender Re-entry', *Crime & Delinquency* 2001 47(3): 428–445. Some critics have referred to the restorative justice idea that victims may play a role in offenders' reentry as 'victims in the service of offenders', see Ashworth (2000), above, n6.
41   See summary in Erez (1999), above, n9.
42   Erez (1999), above, n9.
43   eg, Ashworth (2000), above, n6; Sanders et al (2001), above, n2.
44   For other approaches that combine elements of restorative and adversarial justice see L. Kurkie, 'Incorporating restorative and community justice into American sentencing and corrections', *Sentencing & Corrections: Issues for the 21st Century*, US Department of Justice, Office of Justice Programs: National Institute of Justice, 1999.

The restorative/therapeutic value of the VIS is also evident in other documents that highlight the informational function of the VIS. For instance, an official publication of the US Department of Justice which summarises the gains for victims over the past decade, and describes its agenda for the future, *New Directions from the Field: Victims' Rights and Services for the 21st Century*,[45] maintains that the VIS is a mechanism to inform judges about the crime impact, but it explicitly states: 'It is significant for victims' healing that the judge acknowledge at the time of sentencing that victims have been injured, solicit specific information from victims on the crime's impact on their lives, and explain the terms of the offender's sentence.'[46] This document recognises the restorative function of the VIS in the sentencing context.

The inclusion of the VIS in the repertoire of restorative justice practices underscores the value of the VIS in improving victims' well-being. Beyond the symbolic recognition it provides victims, the VIS is presented at the culmination of the criminal justice process, and at a point where its expressive potential can engage key courtroom participants in the disposition of the crime. As such, the VIS can trigger helpful reactions, and it can evoke appropriate emotions that serve therapeutic ends.[47] The emerging field of therapeutic jurisprudence[48] has considered the VIS as an important reform that can promote the psychological well-being of those engaged in it.[49]

The VIS has therapeutic potential both for victims[50] as well as defendants.[51] It can provide offenders a concrete and unmediated picture of the harm their actions have caused, presenting an opportu-

45   *New Directions from the Field: Victims' Rights and Services for the 21st Century* (US Department of Justice, 1998)

46   Ibid p108.

47   Roberts and Erez (2004), above, n18.

48   eg D. B. Wexler, 'Practicing therapeutic Jurisprudence: psycho-legal soft spots and strategies' in D. P. Stolle, D. B. Wexler, and B. J.Winick (eds), *Practicing Therapeutic Jurisprudence: law as a helping profession*, (Carolina Academic Press, 2000) at pp45–67.

49   eg R. P. Wiebe, 'The Mental Health Implications of Crime Victims' Rights' (1996) In D. B. Wexler and B. J. Winick (eds), *Law in a Therapeutic Key: Developments in Therapeutic Jurisprudence* (Carolina Academic Press, 1996); J. L. Herman, 'The Mental Health of Crime Victims: impact of legal intervention', *Journal of Traumatic Stress*, 2003 16(2):159–166.

50   Erez (1999), above, n9; Herman (2003), ibid.

51   Roberts and Erez (2004), above, n18.

nity for expressing regret or apology.[52] The option to formally submit a VIS constitutes an occasion for communication between the victim and his or her violator, and as such should become a vital legislated right. Exchanges between victims and offenders, which a VIS can invoke, enhance offenders' understanding of the consequences of their acts, and increase victims' familiarity with the offence and the offender's circumstances. Such familiarity can reduce victims' punitiveness, and help offenders in taking responsibility for their actions.[53] Victims who wish to provide input into sentencing about their harm should be afforded the option to submit VIS, even in circumstances in which the VIS may be 'irrelevant' due to a negotiated plea or a mandatory sentence which does not leave judges discretion regarding the sentence.[54]

Victim voice and placing impact information before the court

The substantive character of the right for 'victim voice' has implications for the way victim impact information should be placed before the court. Concerns about potential violations of defendant rights may arise in this context, as VIS may be prejudicial, inflammatory, or include new issues that are not part of the record. Research has shown, however, that these situations are not frequent, nor do they present a serious threat to defendant rights that cannot be prevented or corrected.[55]

Self-administered VIS forms in which victims write the information without professional assistance, reflect the true voice of the victim.[56] However, a drawback of this method is that some victims may insert expressions that are irrelevant or inadmissible. If justice

---

52 C. J. Petrucci, 'Apology in Criminal Justice Setting: evidence for including apology as an additional component in the legal system', *Behavioral Science and the Law* 2002 20: 337–362.

53 Roberts and Erez (2004), above, n18.

54 See for instance M. Cole (2003), 'Perceptions of the use of Victim Impact Statements in Canada: a survey of Crown Counsel in Ontario', MA Thesis, University of Ottawa; J. V. Roberts and A. Edgar (2002), 'Victim Impact Statements and Sentencing: perceptions of the Judiciary', Policy Center for Victim Issues, Department of Justice, Ottawa, Canada.

55 See Erez (1999), above, n9.

56 They are also less costly, which is another important consideration in adopting measures in criminal justice.

officials prepare the statement, they will screen out such information. But VIS prepared by officials may not reflect accurately the victims' feelings, or incorporate their exact wording in describing the crime impact. As justice officials (particularly if overburdened with other responsibilities) tend to present victim harm in generic terms or rush through the 'extra' work,[57] VIS prepared by professionals may not reflect the victim's voice.[58] Having victims who are interested and capable, prepare their own statements may help in accomplishing the benefits of expression through writing,[59] with justice officials ascertaining that the communication does not incorportate any abuse of the right for input or violate defendant rights.

The manner in which the content of VIS is conveyed to the court also impacts on the meaning of voice. Some countries (eg, US and Canada) require that the VIS is submitted (in writing or orally) by the victim. Other countries (eg, England and Wales) rely on prosecutors to communicate the content of the VIS to the court. Experience has shown that when prosecutors convey the impact statement, they are inclined to edit, withhold or 'lose' information, particularly if the interests of the prosecutor are not aligned with those of the victim.[60] The tendency of legal professionals to 'sanitise' victim impact information, especially when they think the statement is exaggerated, has been documented.[61] Having interested victims present their statements may be another way to prevent the undermining of the VIS aims.

The benefits of VIS and reconciling victim and defendant rights

Victim and defendant rights are not necessarily in conflict with respect to submission of the VIS; they may even be compatible in regards to its restorative justice aims. Presenting the VIS in open

57   eg, Erez and Rogers, 'Victim Impact Statements and Sentencing Outcomes and Processes: the perspectives of legal professionals', *Br J Criminol* 1999 39(2): 216–239.

58   Roberts and Erez (2004), above, n18.

59   See M. J. A. Schoutrop, A. Lange, G. Hanewald, U. Davidovich and H. Salomon, 'Structured writing and processing major stressful events: a controlled trial', *Psychotherapy and Psychosomatics* 2002 71(3): 151–157.

60   Erez (1999), above, n9.

61   Erez and Rogers (1999), above, n57.

court facilitates victim-offender communication, which is commonly absent in adversarial proceedings. Encouraging victim-offender communication in open court through the VIS can produce the benefits of reconciliation programs[62] – opportunity for offenders to accept responsibility or express remorse directly to the victim. These programs also allow victims, who wish to remain in the formal and protective setting of the courtroom, the opportunity of expressing their feelings about the victimisation, without having to meet offenders outside the court.[63]

Because adversarial proceedings allow a limited opportunity for communication between victims and offenders, the victim's delivering of the VIS may acquire special significance. The victim is ideally placed to sensitise the offender to the consequences of the crime.[64] Offenders would be more likely to appreciate a victim presentation of harm than they would relate to impact details presented by the prosecutor. Because victims and offenders are usually not familiar with legal jargon or procedures, and often share a similar backgound,[65] a direct appeal by the victim to the offender may constitute a more effective way to make offenders reflect on their actions. Impact information delivered by the victim is more likely to be met with the defendant's apology and acceptance of responsibility.[66] Research suggests that victims can be empowered by their ability to confer or withhold forgiveness, and that victims' aggressive feelings are likely to be attenuated following genuine requests for forgiveness.[67]

Not all victims present in court during sentencing will exercise the right to speak. Fear of public speaking, fear of the defendant, or just not having the need to express oneself may be reasons for which victims would be reluctant to speak in open court. A sizeable proportion of victims nevertheless wish to make use of this right.[68] Research in the United States, Australia and Canada confirms that victims have

---

62 Kurkie (1999), above, n44.
63 Wemmers (2002), above, n25.
64 Roberts and Erez (2004), above, n18.
65 A. Sanders, 'Victim Participation in an Exclusionary Criminal Justice System' in C. Hoyle and R. Young, *New Visions of Crime Victims*, (Hart, 2002) at p197.
66 Roberts and Erez (2004), above, n18.
67 C. J. Petrucci, (2002), above, n52.
68 eg, E. Villmoare and V. Neto (1987), 'Victim appearances at sentencing hearings under California's Bill of Rights', US Department of Justice, Washington DC. Roberts and Edgar (2002), above, n54, found that providing victim allocution rights did not increase the number of victims who want to speak in court, but they found that there is a portion that is interested in doing so.

an interest in communicating with the offender[69] thereby benefitting from restorative justice elements in adversarial proceedings.

Victims should therefore have an opportunity to speak at sentencing, and delivering the VIS in their own words should be a vital part of any attempt to integrate victims in proceedings. Abuse of the opportunity for input and use of inappropriate language by either victims or offenders, would warrant court intervention and prevention of the communication. These circumstances should not be used as reasons to deny victim input rights.[70]

The VIS also creates an opportunity for the court to communicate State recognition of the harm that victims have suffered, confirming that they have been wronged. If the victim is in court, the sentencing judge has the opportunity to speak directly to the victim and to validate his or her harm. Victims who found their own words quoted in judges' sentencing remarks highly appreciated it and reported higher satisfaction with justice.[71]

Judges are commonly aware of their power to recognise victims as the injured party, and that referring to the VIS in sentencing remarks may enhance victims' feelings as being recognised. Research suggests that judges appreciate the therapeutic value of such references or quotes, and often make use of them in court.[72] There is no violation of defendant rights by judges validating victims' pain or injury through quoting the VIS.[73]

Conclusion

Research has documented that the right to be heard at various points in the criminal justice process is important to crime victims. Most victims are interested in participating in the justice process, and they want an opportunity to tell, in their own words, the way that the crime has affected them. Court procedures rarely provide victims with an

---

69   See Erez (1999), above, n9; Roberts and Edgar (2002), above, n54; Cole (2003), above n54.

70   Roberts and Erez (2004), above, n18.

71   See Erez (1999), above, n9.

72   Research in Australia (see Erez and Rogers (1999), above n57 and Canada (see Roberts and Edgar, 2002) confirms that judges recognise this power and make use of it when the opportunity arises. Crown Prosecutors in Canada attested to this fact as well. See Cole (2003), above, n69.

73   Roberts and Edgar, 2003; Roberts and Erez (2004), above, n18.

opportunity to construct a coherent and meaningful narrative.[74] The VIS represents a means to provide victims with a voice at sentencing and allow them to express the impact of the crime on their lives. In adversarial legal systems the VIS is the only tool by which victims can articulate their suffering, identify their concerns and communicate the way their lives have been affected by the crime.

There is evidence to show that the VIS can serve therapeutic ends, particularly if judges validate the harm sustained by victims. VIS properly administered can serve restorative justice purposes for both victims and offenders. Instead of attempting to 'legalise' restorative justice schemes,[75] it would be preferable to consider ways to 'restorise' adversarial justice systems. Integrating victim voice through a VIS is one such avenue.

Research findings about the benefits of VIS for victims as well as offenders point to the value of moving in this direction. Legal professionals' co-operation with the reform purpose and spirit is likely to bear fruit in the form of victim and offender satisfaction. A co-ordinated and concerted effort by legal professionals to inform victims about the role of the VIS in criminal proceedings (eg, prosecutors or those who assist victims re-orient victims in the direction of communicating with the offender in addition to the court) or judges' validation of victim input in their sentencing remarks, could help in accomplishing this goal. Redirecting prevailing court approaches to VIS from an informational tool for the court to its expressive or communicative role for victims would assist all parties involved.

Ultimately, it is our underlying value system and ideology, not data, that will determine whether victims are meaningfully integrated into proceedings. The road to incorporating a victim voice in adversarial proceedings has not been smooth. Nor has it been free of pockets of resistance and neglect.[76] Attempts to integrate victims outside the adverarial justice system through restorative justice schemes have worked for some victims; but they have not served the many who wish to remain within the protective structure of adversarial systems. For them, a VIS properly implemented may become a viable solution. The perception of victims as 'Barbarians at the gates'[77] combined with politically correct arguments concerning 'defendants'

---

74 Herman (2003), above, n49. See also Roberts and Erez, forthcoming.

75 Ashworth (2002), above, n2.

76 See *New Directions for the 21st Century* (1998) at chapter 3. Above, n45.

77 See P. G. Cassell 'Barbarians at the Gates? A reply to the critics of the victims rights amendment', *Utah Law Review* 1999 (2): 437–539.

rights' have been used for too long by unsympathetic, if not hostile, legal cultures of adversarial systems to deny victims the right to be heard.[78] There is sufficient data to show the inadequacy of these arguments. A careful reading of the research would call for rethinking prevailing ideologies that restorative justice principles and adversarial proceedings cannot be reconciled when it comes to integrating a victim voice in sentencing.[79]

78   P. G. Cassell (1999) reviewing the curriculum of law schools in the US noted the absence of materials related to victims, their plight, and interests. He submits that this void helps in propagating the legal culture that is hostile to victims. The enormous difficulties in engaging law schools in discussions about integrating victim related study materials are described in the September 2003 publication of the Office of Victims of Crime, US Department of Justice, *Learning About Victims of Crime: A Training Model for Victim Service Providers and Allied Professionals.*

79   See also W. T. Pizzi 'Victims' Rights: rethinking our adversary system', *Utah Law Review* 1999 (2): 349–367.

CHAPTER 8

Involving victims in sentencing: a conflict with defendants' rights?

By Andrew Sanders

Allen & Overy Professor of Criminal Law and Criminology,
University of Manchester

This volume looks at how far the rights of victims can be reconciled with those of the accused. There are good reasons for framing the debate in this way. We are used to the idea that accused people have the right to be presumed innocent until proven guilty, or not to be sentenced for crimes that have not been proven. But does the victim not have an interest in these matters too? Until very recently, the concerns and interests of victims have been neglected in all Western democracies. Now that the language of 'rights' and, in particular, 'human rights', has become pervasive, especially since the Human Rights Act was passed in 1998, it seems logical to confer rights on victims too. Thus many commentators implicitly criticise the fact that what we may loosely call 'rights' under the Victims Charter and subsequent developments are not 'legal rights' at all in the sense of being enforceable. Some go as far as to argue that victims have human rights on a par with those of the accused, and draw on judgements of the ECHR to support this view.[1] And some – Edna Erez for example – argue that victims should indeed have rights in relation to sentencing.[2]

Andrew Ashworth argues that we should recognise the human rights of victims as well as those of the accused.[3] However, he is alive to the problem that the rights of victims – whether 'human rights' or

---

1 See especially, *Doorson v Netherlands* (1996) 22 EHRR 330.
2 See page 81.
3 A. Ashworth, *The Criminal Process: an evaluative study* (OUP, 1998).

not – are or might be, in some circumstances, irreconcilable with those of the accused. He therefore argues that enforceable rights for victims should be confined to 'substantive' rights (such as to information about their cases, where there is no clash of interests) and should not extend to 'procedural' rights (such as involvement in the trial and sentencing process). Those of us who agree that the presumption of innocence is of paramount importance and who seek to reduce, rather than inflate, sentencing levels, may pragmatically agree with this position. The problem is that there is no principle on which one can ground it. If we grant victims rights in one respect, why not in another? The mere fact of pre-existing rights of the accused is no answer, for the absence of pre-existing rights for victims is part of the problem, and cannot therefore be used as a justification for a continuation of the pre-eminence of protections for the accused.

One way around the problem is to seek to deny victims legal rights altogether. But how can we do that now that we recognise that the concerns and interests of victims have been *unjustly* neglected? The answer is to argue primarily for the *social* rights of victims instead. In this paper I shall do this on the basis that this will benefit victims and the accused. The paper is concerned specifically with sentencing, and with victim impact statements in particular. But the argument – that victims should have only limited legal rights, and certainly no human rights – at this stage of the criminal process is applicable to other stages as well.

A zero sum game?

Arguments around the rights of victims often have a curiously schizophrenic quality. For example, governments increasingly use the past neglect of the rights of victims as a justification for eroding the rights of the accused. At the time of writing (September 2003) the current criminal justice bill is a prime example. Elements of this bill such as the undermining of the double jeopardy rule and the relaxation of rules restricting the use of evidence of previous convictions erode many due process principles. The government claims that this is part of its new policy of putting victims 'at the heart of the system' – that there is, in other words, a zero sum game, whereby rights for the accused have to be traded off against rights for victims, and vice versa. But as Jackson shows,[4] these rules that protect the accused generally

4   See page 65.

do so in order to guard against wrongful convictions. It cannot possibly help victims if, as a result of this bill undermining the rights of the accused, the wrong people are convicted, leaving the real criminals free to victimise yet others. The opposition set up between the rights of victims and those of the accused is therefore often a false conflict.

On the other hand, there are sometimes genuine conflicts between the rights of the two groups. Take the restriction in sexual offences trials on the use of sexual history evidence introduced in the Youth Justice and Criminal Evidence Act 1999.[5] This was clearly introduced, with some justification, to help victims. For not only had evidence of victims' sexual history (both with the defendant and others) often undermined the prosecution case, despite its dubious relevance, but also the character assassination which its use entailed was highly distressing for many victims. The result was, in many cases, 'secondary victimisation'. The reform was clearly an attempt to enhance 'fair trial' rights[6] for victims of sexual offences. However, a commonly used defence to rape is that the defendant believed (however irrationally) that the victim was consenting. Thus any restriction, such as this one, on the evidence a defendant could use to support a claim that he so believed (eg that the victim had consented to sexual relations in similar circumstances in the past) inevitably undermined *the defendant's* right to a fair trial. Here there is indeed a zero sum game. It is impossible to construct rules that provide for fair trial equally to victims and defendants where sexual history evidence is concerned – as was recognised in the first case on this reform.[7] Yet the change in law had originally been presented by government as though the rights of rape victims could be enhanced in this way without undermining the fair trial rights of the accused.

Libertarians are sometimes similarly schizophrenic, but in the opposite way. Organisations such as JUSTICE and Liberty (and, indeed, LAG) fight measures such as the criminal justice bill on precisely the grounds highlighted by Jackson: that eroding the rights of suspects as in that bill does not necessarily enhance the rights of victims. Yet these organisations' understandable empathy for less powerful groups, such as the victims of sexual abuse, lead them to sometimes turn a blind eye to the zero sum game even when it stares them in the eyes – the sexual history evidence measures in the Youth Justice and Criminal Evidence Act 1999 being a clear example.

---

5   section 41.
6   *Doorson v Netherlands* (1996) 22 EHRR 330.
7   *R v A (No 2)* [2001] 2 Cr App R 351.

What about victim involvement in sentencing? This probably increases the severity of punishment. While the evidence from the UK and other jurisdictions is not conclusive on this,[8] it is highly unlikely to lower sentencing levels except perhaps in the context of restorative justice. If victim involvement does lead to more severe punishment, is this an example of the zero sum problem? Well, yes, in a way: the more that is done for victims in this way the more severely, on average, defendants will be punished. The less that is done for victims, the less severely defendants will be punished. But no one could argue that this is a clash of *rights*. Sentencing in the UK is highly discretionary, so – within a broad range – defendants do not have the *right* to a less, as distinct from a more, severe sentence.

Thus if our worry is simply one of reconciling the legal rights of victims and the accused, then as far as victim involvement in sentencing is concerned the answer is that there is no clash of rights. Let victim involvement, through victim impact statements or any other means, develop at will. However, if we are concerned about *justice* – for victims and the accused – then we do have to be concerned with the way in which apparently enhancing the position of one group may be done at the expense of the other. The trick is to find a way of enhancing the position of victims in sentencing so that it is not at the expense of the accused. In other words, to transform this from a zero sum problem to a 'win-win' situation.

Victim Impact Statements: their nature and rationale

We have seen that, until recently, victims have been completely uninvolved in sentencing, but we need to ask why is that is a problem. What are the purposes of victim participation?

- To give victims a 'voice', to the extent, some advocates argue, of 'empowering' victims;
- to enable the interests and/or views of victims to be taken into account in decision-making, increasing the relevant information available to sentencers;
- to increase the probability that victims will be treated with respect

---

8   For reviews of the literature, see L. Sebba, *Third Parties: Victims and the Criminal Justice System* (1996); A. Sanders, *Taking Account of Victims in the Criminal Justice System: A Review of the Literature* (Scottish Office, 1999).

by criminal justice agencies, reducing the stress of criminal proceedings for them; and

- to increase victim satisfaction with the criminal justice system,
making them more likely to co-operate with criminal justice
agencies.

Victim impact statement (VIS) schemes developed in the 1970s and
1980s in the USA and have now spread through the common law
world. VIS provide information about the effects of offences on victims and, where appropriate, on victims' close family members. Such
effects may be physical, financial, psychological, or emotional. The
information is provided by victims to the police, prosecuting agency
and/or court, to be used as those agencies think fit in relation to sentencing decisions (among others). As far as sentencing is concerned,
the VIS may be presented directly by the victim (usually through
the prosecutor) or via agencies such as the police or probation services. *Impact* statements provide factual information, while *opinion*
statements (VOS) give the views of victims about one or more of
these decisions. Although some US States allow VOS, VIS are more
common.

The Victims' Charter Pilot VIS Scheme and after

The 1996 Victims' Charter announced that victim impact statements
(VIS) would be experimentally piloted in England and Wales for a
wide range of cases. However, as we shall see, significant types of case
were excluded from the scheme. The pilot projects began in 1997 in
six police force areas. Nearly one third of eligible victims opted to provide a VIS. There were two evaluations. In the first, over 100 victims
who provided a VIS, and over 50 who had not, were interviewed. Of
those who opted in, a majority had 'expressive' reasons for doing so,
and a majority also had instrumental reasons for doing so (many
expressing both types of reason). We attempted to gauge how far victims really did feel empowered, both at the start of their cases and at
the end. Seventy seven per cent of participants were pleased that they
participated at the start (only two per cent being displeased, the rest
being neutral or not having a clear view) but only 57 per cent were
pleased by the end (20 per cent were displeased).[9] Indeed, while

9   C. Hoyle et al, *Evaluation of the 'One Stop Shop' and Victim Statement Pilot
Projects* (Home Office, 1998).

around 33 per cent of victims who made a statement felt better after-wards, around 18 per cent felt worse. This is hardly a triumph of empowerment.

Some victims were dissatisfied because they did not say all that they had wanted to say in the VIS (bearing in mind that this was a VIS, not VOS, scheme). For others the situation had changed after making their statements. But the main reason for dissatisfaction was that many victims thought that their statements had been ignored. Eight per cent knew that their statements had been used in court, but 90 per cent did not know to what use, if any, their statement had been put. Although advocates of VIS such as Erez argue that empowerment can be secured through the expressive, as well as instrumental, purpose of VIS, this does not tally with the experience of large numbers of our interviewees. If the major reason why most victims in conventional adversarial systems feel marginalised is that they give one (witness) statement and are then ignored, why should VIS – in which they give two statements and are then ignored – make any difference?

Clearly it was important to discover whether victims were ignored. So the second evaluation examined the use of VIS by prosecutors and courts. Files were examined, and prosecutors, defence lawyers, mag-istrates, court officials and judges were interviewed. Although it seems that few VIS had actually been ignored, equally few had made any difference to sentence (or any other) decisions. Some victims expected their VIS to make a conviction more likely. The lack of real-ism of some of these expectations is obvious to anyone who under-stands the system, but that is precisely the point: many victims do not understand the system, and the process of eliciting VIS does nothing to help them understand it. Even where VIS could make a difference in theory they virtually never did in reality. This was partly because it did not occur to prosecutors that the information might be relevant to bail or prosecution decisions. But it was mostly because, in relation to all these decisions, it was not actually relevant or, if it was, it was not verified. For when victims told judges what they expected to hear they told judges nothing new, and so the sentence was not affected. When victims told judges unexpected things, they had to be 'taken with a pinch of salt' in the absence of supporting evidence. Where a minor assault led to a serious injury, for example, this unexpected impact would normally be taken into account in the sentence, but the judge or magistrate would normally seek medical evidence about the injury rather than rely on the VIS.[10]

10 R. Morgan and A. Sanders, *The Uses of Victim Statements* (Home Office, 1999).

Neither victim dissatisfaction with VIS, nor its causes, is peculiar to the UK. Nor is it a result of the experimental nature of VIS. Similar results have been found in, for example, the USA and Australia.[11] For many victims, being asked to contribute, but then having that contribution ignored, is insulting. Bitterness and resentment about the crime often appears in such cases to be intensified as the process to which victims seek access denies them influence. It gives them a voice but not the dignity that attaches to being heard. As Rod Morgan and I commented in the second Charter evaluation, if the VIS experiment is to be continued, the Charter should be amended to make it clear that information from victims will *not* normally be taken into account by decision makers. This was not entirely facetious. After all, if the main aim of VIS is 'expressive' (ie non-instrumental), why not be open about its lack of instrumental value? In reality, the objectives of VIS are muddled.[12] But even this recognition is to miss the point that, as Paul Rock notes, quoting a Canadian criminal justice official, 'politically, you can't be too nice to victims'.[13] This is equally applicable to the UK in the new millennium. But 'being nice' and actually helping are not necessarily the same things. In 2000, the government decided to introduce a 'Personal Statement Scheme'. Confronted on TV with the findings of Hoyle et al, the responsible government minister repeated the mantra that 'this is what victims want', deliberately ignoring the point that many wanted them only before they were made and then ignored.

The exclusionary way forward: with VIS

The only way in which victims can be made more satisfied while using VIS would be to oblige sentencers to acknowledge VIS. They would either have to take notice of VIS, and to say so in court; or to explain, again in court, why they are not influenced by the VIS. This

---

This research, together with the first evaluation, is summarised in Home Office Research Findings No 107 (1999) and in A. Sanders et al, 'Victim Impact Statements: Don't Work, Can't Work', [2001] Crim LR 447.

11 See L. Sebba, n8, above. See A. Sanders, n8, above.

12 I. Edwards, 'Victim Participation in Sentencing: The Problems of Incoherence' *The Howard Journal* [2001] 40:39.

13 P. Rock, 'Victims' Rights in England and Wales at the Beginning of the 21st Century' in J. Ermisch, D. Gallie and A. Heath (eds), *Social Challenges and Sociological Puzzles* (OUP, 2002).

would be consistent with the general trend towards greater accountability and the giving of reasons. The idea sounds, in principle, unobjectionable. A parallel can be found in the criminal justice bill. This establishes statutory guidelines for minimum 'tariffs' in life sentence cases, and requires judges to state in court why, if they depart from these minima, they choose to do so.

In practice this idea would be highly objectionable. It is one thing for judges to say why they do not think what a government wants should be done in particular cases, but it is quite another to say why victims are wrong. We have seen that the hopes and expectations of many victims are unrealistic, and that much of the information they provide is irrelevant or insufficiently concrete or reliable to be influential. How 'empowering' and cathartic would it be for victims to be told in open court that what they say is unreliable, unrealistic or irrelevant? This would be secondary victimisation with a vengeance. Judges will be naturally reluctant to humiliate victims in this way. Many more than now will therefore take in to account what victims say, thereby increasing sentence severity.

Thus the zero sum game would move into action. In some cases victims and the public would be told openly that what those victims said would be ignored, which would often be hurtful to those victims, while in other cases sentences would be more severe than they would otherwise be, which would be hurtful to the defendants. It is true that, as Erez and Rogers show,[14] VIS has not generally raised sentencing levels, but since this is because VIS are generally ignored by sentencers, and Erez and Rogers castigate them for this, one can only assume that advocates such as Erez are unhappy with this and would support measures on the lines outlined above. While Erez argues for more *accurate* sentencing, as distinct from more *severe* sentencing, very few victims submit VIS that argue for leniency or present facts that point in that direction (this is not to say that victims are generally punitive – simply that non-punitive victims rarely make VIS).

The advocate of VIS would argue that increased sentences would simply enable sentencers to take account of information that should be taken into account anyway, that VIS is a just deserts approach and hence not unjust; and that the more this was done, the less irrelevant information would be provided by victims and the less sentencers would ignore them. This argument can be countered at two levels. First, while it is true that VIS (as distinct from VOS) only provides

14 'Victim impact statements and sentencing outcomes and processes' *BJ Crim* 39: 216.

information on issues that *should* be before the sentencer, it is likely that much of the content of many VIS will continue to be irrelevant and/or unsubstantiated assertion. The danger is that judges will be influenced by such information when they should not be, in an attempt to avoid upsetting victims (in the same way that defence lawyers very rarely challenge the contents of VIS for fear of generating more sympathy for victims and thus creating the opposite effect to that intended).

Second, 'just deserts' is a way of establishing fairness as between different cases – striving towards the similar treatment of cases of similar seriousness and the more severe treatment of more serious cases. It does nothing to establish thresholds (what is the minimum seriousness of a case to warrant imprisonment, for example) nor the steepness of 'punitive ascent' (from fines to community penalties to short custodial sentences and finally to long custodial sentences). In other words, even the entirely proper application of just deserts principles to the use of VIS would do nothing to hold back increasing sentence severity – indeed, it would probably fuel it. At a time when sentencing is escalating anyway, with the prison population doubled in the last ten years, this would be a backward step in terms of justice for offenders.

To try to explain this increasingly harsh and authoritarian penal policy, Garland argues that in late-modern society (that is, the USA and UK from the late 1970s) the legitimacy of penal-welfarism became fatally undermined because of a combination of socio-economic and political change, the failure of the criminal justice system to control crime, and academic critique. Thus the new penal policies focus on the consequences of crime rather than its social causes. These policies conflict and converge as the State seeks to both adapt to its failure (by, for example, seeking crime prevention partnerships and by doing little about less serious offences) and deny that failure. Denial includes what Garland calls policies of 'punitive segregation' for more serious offences, such as 'Three strikes and you're out' and the British equivalents.[15] This gives 'public opinion' the impression that 'something is being done'.[16]

Garland argues that the new victim policies, of which VIS is one,

---

15   See the Crime (Sentences) Act 1997. Measures adopted by the Labour government from this Conservative legislation include the automatic life sentence for second offences of severe violence, and minimum sentences for repeated drugs and domestic burglary offences.

16   D. Garland, *The Culture of Control* (OUP, 2001) at p135.

are central to 'punitive segregation', for at 'the centre of contemporary penal discourse is (a political projection of) the individual victim...'.[17] Because the State can do little about crime, it turns its attention to the consequences of crime – victims in particular. It seeks to show that 'something is being done' for victims by arguing that this is a major objective of punitive segregation, so that even if punitive segregation fails in crime-reduction terms it can be claimed as a success in giving victims what they want (that is, what political projections of them want).

These approaches are 'exclusionary' because, at the most general level, policies of 'punitive segregation' separate 'us' (the supposedly law-abiding majority) from 'them' (the 'criminal' minority). Policies that parade victims as the embodiments of 'us' cast 'them' out even further. Moreover, as Garland observes, as part of the 'something is being done about crime' approach, offenders' rights are eroded: 'A zero sum policy game is assumed wherein the offender's gain is the victim's loss, and being 'for' victims automatically means being tough on offenders'.[18] As Roach puts it, drawing on the similar Canadian experience, 'Victims' rights became the new rights-bearing face of crime control.'[19] But exclusionary policies do not only cast criminals out, both literally and in the sense of no longer 'deserving' human rights. They also exclude *victims*. For as Garland notes, though he does not pursue the point, it is not the interests and voices of individual victims, or even victims' groups, that are sought in these new policies, but a political projection of those victims. It is for this reason that in both Britain and Northern Ireland, Victim Support has been careful not to join in the zero sum game, and has not sought participatory rights of a decision-making kind. But none of this has prevented the government from announcing ever-more punitive policies in the name of victims.

VIS and its variants are probably more popular with people who have never used them than with those who have. They are good for idealised victims, rather than for real victims. Even supporters of VIS, such as Erez, acknowledge raised expectations, resulting dissatisfaction and the inevitably limited impact of VIS on decision-making, although they do not let this obstruct their advocacy of such schemes.[20] VIS provides solace for people who feel they could be the

17   ibid, p144.

18   ibid, p11.

19   K. Roach, *Due Process and Victim's Rights* (Toronto University Press, 1999) at p32.

20   For another example, see E. Erez, 'Integrating a Victim Perspective in Criminal

next victim. As potential victims outnumber real victims (at least, real victims of serious crimes), this is a good vote-winner even if dissatisfaction with these schemes is blamed on the officials who design and implement them. Dissatisfaction also doubtless amplifies the anger and hurt already felt towards the offender, thus increasing the victim-offender gap and doing nothing to reduce the exclusion of victims or offenders from 'normal' society.

Differentiation only works if a minority of society are the 'bad' criminals (the Other), leaving the majority to be 'good' victims and potential victims. Thus the majority of crimes – and thus the majority of victims – are ignored. Everyday fraud (such as thefts of work materials and deceptions such as tax evasion and expense fiddles), everyday traffic offences, accidents at work, and so forth are all excluded from political projections of 'real' crimes and 'real' victims. Indeed this is true at a legal level too, as these crimes are excluded from the Victims' Charter VIS scheme (and its successor). The victim of criminal damage can demand retribution but the victim of a pollution or work-safety offence cannot.

VIS thus embodies a triple exclusion: of certain types of offence, offender and victim; of 'real' criminals by differentiating them from the rest of 'us' in order to justify ever-more severe punishments; and of victims from the criminal process by raising their expectations and then frequently dashing them – giving them two 'bites' of a sour cherry is little better than giving them one. VIS is the most striking manifestation of Garland's argument that victim policy facilitates differentiation (of the 'bad' from the 'unfortunate') and the 'criminology of the other' that justifies punitive segregation and intensifies the exclusionary tendencies of late-modern society.

The inclusionary way forward: non-decision-making involvement

Inclusive approaches reject the zero sum game, and argue that the interests of victims and offenders can and should be pursued together. Rather than the idealised interests and views of 'straw women' victims being used to legitimate punitive segregation, the *actual* interests and views of individual victims would be used to assist reintegration – of both victims and offenders – to the extent that is

Justice Through Victim Impact Statements' in A. Crawford and J. Goodey (eds), *Integrating a Victim Perspective Within Criminal Justice* (Ashgate, 2000).

possible, financially prudent, and necessary. This does not describe any system in the present or past of which I am aware. Shapland, for example, argues for 'criminal justice as a public service' because she sees that neither victims nor offenders are central to the concerns of criminal justice as currently practised.[21] It is true that some restorative justice approaches are based on principles of inclusion and do occupy a space (albeit usually marginal) in most modern penal systems. The main problem with restorative justice, as advocated by many of its proselytisers, is that it tends to assume that the opinions, rights and interests of victims and offenders are always reconcilable. This is untenable. We therefore need to think of ways of making existing criminal justice processes, that do not rely on restorative justice, more inclusionary than they are at present.

The aim of victim participation within an inclusionary approach would be to give effect to the views of victims where this would increase the overall effectiveness of criminal justice. Also, where applicable, it would aim to help victims to understand why their views are not given effect – where, for example, to do so would conflict with the rights of defendants. This would be in order to reduce secondary victimisation by increasing victim satisfaction with the system and to reduce the exclusionary 'us' and 'them' gap. There is a limit to how much can be explained by letter or phone, or even in person, to someone who has not experienced the process in question. In other words, victims who do not participate in some way in decision making are less likely than those who do participate to fully understand what happened and why.

Inquisitorial systems, for example, allow far more participation on the part of victims than do adversarial systems.[22] Victims are often entitled to ask judges to put questions to the accused, may give a full oral account of the impact of the crime on them, and may express their views. While it is not generally believed that victim participation in inquisitorial systems affects decisions any more than it does in adversarial systems, understanding is increased through participation, dialogue and sight of the material on the basis of which decisions are made. What little research there is suggests that victim satisfaction is, as a result, relatively high in inquisitorial systems with direct partici-

---

21 J. Shapland, 'Creating responsible criminal justice agencies' in A. Crawford and J. Goodey (ed), *Integrating a victim perspective within criminal justice* (Ashgate, 2000). Note that she expresses great surprise at what she sees, and does not use the terms 'inclusionary' or 'exclusionary'.

22 A. Sanders, *Taking Account of Victims in the Criminal Justice System* (Scottish Office, 1999).

pation.[23] This type of approach, along with restorative justice where appropriate, could be adapted for a UK context.[24]

Tyler has argued that when offenders understand the process and see it as legitimate they are more ready to accept outcomes that they regard as unjust.[25] This should apply equally to victims. Thus, whether through restorative justice or inquisitorial-style victim participation, increased dialogue and understanding should reduce secondary victimisation and thus increase 'freedom'.[26] So far, government has resisted developing victim policy on these lines, for reasons that are not clear. If it continues to do so, we may justifiably conclude that victims are being used in the service of exclusion rather than in an attempt to satisfy their legitimate concerns. For this approach could be a 'win-win' situation in which offenders receive, where appropriate, *less* severe sentences and victims could emerge no less satisfied than now and, one would hope, often more satisfied. It is true that the 'direct communication with victims' initiative developed recently by the CPS is a step in this direction. But it only applies to serious cases (not including the types of case excluded from the Victims' Charter), and does so only when charges are dropped or downgraded. Nor does it provide genuine involvement or even much discussion. It is therefore a very small step in the right direction.

The approach being advocated is based on the aspiration that when people and institutions, even with different experiences and interests, all aspire to a similar goal – that amorphous ideal of justice – some kind of meeting place will usually be possible. But this is a fragile possibility in many cases. The assertion of rights is often guaranteed to polarise and to shatter fragility, rather than enhancing compromise, understanding and the preservation of a narrow common ground. Thus even in the fraught area of complaints against the police, informal conciliation has been found to be better for both sides in many cases than formal grievance procedures. A restorative approach is suitable in many different fora.[27] This is why the provision of hard

---

23 See especially, E. Erez and E. Bienkowska, 'Victim Participation in Proceedings and Satisfaction with Justice in Continental Systems: The Case of Poland', *Jo Criminal Justice* (1993) 21: 47.

24 A. Sanders et al, 'Victim Impact Statements: Don't Work, Can't Work' [2001] Crim LR 447.

25 T. Tyler, *Why Do People Obey the Law?* (Yale University Press, 1990).

26 A 'freedom' approach which attempts to reconcile the rights of victims with those of the accused across the whole criminal justice board is set out in A. Sanders and R. Young, *Criminal Justice* (Butterworths, 2000), especially chapter 1.

27 J. Braithwaite, *Restorative Justice and Responsive Regulation* (OUP, 2002).

legal rights – still less human rights – for victims would be a backward step. It is not that they, and their rights, are less important than the accused person and his or her rights. It is that, ultimately, it is the accused who risks losing freedom, and therefore deserves guarantees, while the victim hopes to gain freedom by involvement and therefore deserves the opportunity to gain understanding. The two groups have different things at stake that are best achievable by different means. To pretend they are the same does neither a service.

CHAPTER 9

Human rights and victims[1]

By Francesca Klug
*Professorial Research Fellow, Centre for the Study of Human Rights,
London School of Economics*

Victims are at the centre of human rights thinking. No other group of
individuals has a more sacred place in human rights law. Article 34 of
the European Convention on Human Rights (ECHR) grants the right
of petition to anyone claiming to be a 'victim' of a violation of the
Convention. The Optional Protocol of the International Covenant on
Civil and Political Rights (ICCPR) allows the UN's Human Rights
Committee to receive communications from 'victims' of transgres-
sions of the ICCPR. The Human Rights Act 1998, s7, allows an individual who is a 'victim' of 'an unlawful act of a public authority' to take
that authority to court.

The UN is currently in the process of debating 'draft basic Principles and Guidelines' for victims of violations of international human
rights and humanitarian law. These affirm that 'victims should be
treated with compassion and respect for their dignity, have their right
of access to justice and redress mechanisms fully respected . . . together with the expeditious development of appropriate rights and
remedies . . .'[2] This follows a number of 'soft law' initiatives and reso-
lutions on victims by the UN and Council of Europe since the 1980s.[3]

1   With special thanks to Claire O'Brien, research officer at the Centre for the
    Study of Human Rights, for meticulous research.
2   *Draft basic Principles and Guidelines on the right to a remedy and reparation for
    victims of violations of international human rights and humanitarian law,* Annex
    to UN Doc E/CN, 4/2000/62, 18 January, 2000.
3   For example, UNGA Resolution, *Declaration of Basic Principles of Justice
    for Victims of Crime and Abuse of Power,* UN Doc A/RES/40/34, 29.11.95;
    Recommendation No R(85)11 of the Committee of Ministers to Member States

Most significantly, the Preamble to the Rome Statute, which established the new International Criminal Court (ICC), put justice for victims at the heart of its work. Echoing the sentiments in the Universal Declaration of Human Rights, drafted half a century earlier, it recalls that 'during this century millions of children, women and men have been victims of unimaginable atrocities that deeply shock the conscience of humanity'. The statute expressly recognises that measures to guarantee the safety, physical and psychological well-being, dignity and privacy of victims, witnesses and their families are essential to the work of the ICC. The prosecutor is required to take special measures to protect victims and witnesses[4] and the views and concerns of victims must be presented and considered at appropriate stages in the proceedings.[5]

Human rights abuses by private parties under international law

The factor which distinguishes this focus on victims' rights in human rights law from the preoccupation of the current government with ' re-balancing the criminal just system' – most people would assume – is that human rights law is focused on *state* violations whereas the government is obsessed with crimes committed by *individuals*. The campaigns and comments of the main civil liberties NGOs in this country reinforce the impression that within the criminal justice system it is the rights of suspects, defendants and prisoners that human rights law is solely concerned with (though not, interestingly enough, Victim Support, which impressively recognises the potential of the Human Rights Act (HRA) for securing victims' rights).[6] But is this assumption correct, either as a matter of law or discourse? There are various references in the Rome Statute which strongly imply that the ICC has jurisdiction over so-called 'non-state actors' who carry out 'crimes against humanity' and allied abuses against civilian populations.[7]

---

on the position of the victim in the framework of criminal law and procedure, 28.6.85.

4   Article 54(1).
5   Article 68(3).
6   See Human Rights Act 1998 Briefing Paper, Victim Support, 2003.
7   *Rome Statute* Article 7(2)(a)–(e) and 2(f).

The 'draft basic Principles and Guidelines' for victims of violations of international rights law likewise requires victims to be afforded 'equal and effective access to justice *irrespective of who may be the ultimate bearer of responsibility for the violation*'.[8] [emphasis added.]

The UN Convention on the Elimination of All Forms of Discrimination Against Women requires states to take appropriate and effective measures to overcome all forms of gender-based violence, '*whether by public or private act*'.[9] [emphasis added.] There are parallel obligations on states to protect individuals from abuse by private parties under the UN Convention on the Elimination of Racial Discrimination and in the Convention on the Rights of the Child.[10]

Obligations on states under ECHR

More significant, perhaps, for a country like the UK which has incorporated the ECHR into its law, is the evolving jurisprudence of the European Court of Human Rights (ECtHR). It is nearly 20 years since the Court declared that:

> there may be positive obligations [on the state] inherent in an effective respect for private or family life. These obligations may involve the adoption of measures designed to secure respect for private life even in the sphere of the *relations of individuals between themselves*.[11] [emphasis added.]

It is more than 10 years since the then European Commission on Human Rights held that the state was subject to a 'positive obligation' to provide adequate protection for a woman facing sustained sexual harassment by her ex-partner.[12] This protection cannot necessarily be provided by civil remedies.

> . . . Where fundamental values and essential aspects of private life are at stake [as in sexual assaults] effective deterrence . . . can be achieved only by criminal law.[13]

---

8 See above, n1, Article 3(c).

9 CEDAW General Recommendation No. 19, 29.1.92 (para 24).

10 eg CERD Articles 2 (d), Article 4 and Article 6, and CRC Articles 2(2), 3(2), and 19.

11 *X & Y v Netherlands* [1985] 8 EHRR 235. In *Plattform Artze fur das Leben v Austria* [1991] 13 EHRR 204, para 32, the Court declared that 'like Article 8, Article 11 sometimes requires positive measures to be taken, even in the sphere of relations between individuals, if need be'.

12 *Whiteside v UK*, App no 20357/92.

13 *X & Y v Netherlands*, above, n11 at para 27.

There is no direct reference to 'positive obligations' in the ECHR but the ECtHR has founded the doctrine on the basis of two substantive provisions of the Convention. First, the very first Article requires states to secure ECHR rights to everyone in their jurisdiction (not just refrain from abusing them). The Court has concluded that to be secured, rights have to be ' practical and effective' and not ' theoretical or illusory.'[14] In other words, it is no good having a right to life if the state does nothing to deter people from murdering you or fails to adequately investigate such a crime.

Second, Article 13 provides that *effective* remedies should be provided for arguable breaches of Convention rights. The ECtHR's case law has in effect established that the state's obligation to provide 'effective remedies' for violations of fundamental rights by private parties can be met through criminal and domestic law, adequately and sensitively administered. It is only when the state fails to provide such remedies that it has breached the ECHR.[15]

By 1998 the ECtHR was arguing in the contentious but authoritative case of *Osman v UK* that preventative *legislation* is not always enough; preventative *operational measures* may also be necessary to protect the fundamental rights of one individual threatened by another:

> It is common ground that the State's obligation [under Article 2, the right to life] . . . extends beyond its primary duty to secure the right to life by putting in place effective criminal law provisions to deter the commission of offences against the person backed up by law-enforcement machinery for the prevention, suppression and sanctioning of breaches of such provisions. It is thus accepted . . . that Article 2 . . . may also imply in certain well-defined circumstances a positive obligation on the authorities to take preventative operational measures to protect an individual *whose life is at risk from the criminal acts of another individual*.[16] [emphasis added.]

This said, the scope of a state's 'positive obligation' to secure Convention rights violated by private parties is still far from settled. What is

---

14   *Artico v Italy* [1981] 3 EHRR 1, para 33. See also *Soering v UK* [1989] 11 EHRR 439, para 87.

15   eg *X & Y v Netherlands*, above, n11.

16   *Osman v UK* [1999] EHRLR 228, para 115. The court went on to say that this operational duty must not be interpreted to put an impossible or disproportionate burden on state authorities (and must still respect other individuals' Convention rights, eg under Articles 5 and 8). See also *T v UK*; *V v UK* [1999] 30 EHRR 121, '. . . states have a duty . . . to take measures for the protection of the public from violent crimes'.

certain is that it extends to vulnerable victims and potential victims of serious crime who are entitled to special protection, in particular children:

> Sexual abuse is unquestionably an abhorrent type of wrongdoing with debilitating affects on its victim. Children and other vulnerable individuals are entitled to State protection, in the form of effective deterrents from such grave types of interference with essential aspects of their private lives.[17]

It was this line of reasoning which led the European Court of Human Rights to find that the regular severe beating of a child by his stepfather was a breach of Article 3, which prohibits torture and inhuman or degrading treatment and which states have a responsibility to protect against.[18]

For crimes affecting fundamental rights like life and freedom from torture, the ECtHR has also established a duty on the state to respond promptly, diligently and effectively, with official investigations backed up by criminal prosecutions.[19] This includes identifying possible witnesses, questioning suspects sufficiently early on and searching for corroborative evidence.[20] The police, in other words, had a 'positive obligation' to resolutely investigate Stephen Lawrence's murder and patently failed to do so.

In the last few years the ECtHR has extended the state's positive obligation to include the protection of victims and vulnerable witnesses in the court room. In a landmark case in 1996, the ECtHR extended its interpretation of Article 6, primarily concerned with the rights of defendants in criminal proceedings, to take account of the rights of vulnerable witnesses and defendants.

> It is true that Article 6 does not explicitly require the interests of witnesses in general, and those of victims called upon to testify in particular, to be taken into consideration. However their life, liberty or security of person may be at stake, as may interests coming generally with in the ambit of Article 8 [right to a private life]. Such interests of witnesses and victims are in principle protected by other, substantive provisions of the Convention, which imply that Contracting States should organise their criminal proceedings in

17 *Stubbings v UK* [1996] 23 EHRR 213, para 62.

18 *A v UK* (1998) 2 FLR 959.

19 *Aksoy v Turkey* [1996] 23 EHRR 553; *Aydin v Turkey* [1997] 25 EHRR 251; *Kaya v Turkey* [1998] 28 EHRR 1; *Kurt v Turkey* [1998] 27 EHRR 373.

20 *Aksoy v Turkey*, above, n19.

such a way that those interests are not unjustifiably imperilled. Against this background, *principles of fair trial also require that in appropriate cases the interests of the defence are balanced against those of witnesses or victims called upon to testify.*[21] [emphasis added.]

Where necessary, screens and other equipment can be used in court to protect vulnerable witnesses.[22] Recognition has been give to the special features involved in sexual offence crimes like rape. 'In the assessment of the question whether or not in such proceedings an accused received a fair trial, account must be taken of the right to respect for the victim's private life.'[23]

It is not necessarily unfair in such cases, according to a determination by the former European Commission on Human Rights (ECmHR), to prevent the accused cross-examining vulnerable witnesses (including the complainant) provided there are other safeguards in place such as corroborating evidence or appropriate directions from the judge.[24]

However, there has been no ECHR jurisprudence to date to support victims' demands to directly influence sentencing . A complaint by Mrs McCourt that she was not able to participate in the sentencing process of her daughter's murderer was struck out as manifestly unfounded by the former Commission. In their response the ECmHR did note that although there is no right for victims to be involved in Parole Board decisions in the UK, the Home Office does allow the Board to hear victim-submissions.[25]

What's gone wrong with human rights discourse?

So if victims are at the heart of human rights thinking why is it commonly assumed that human rights law is

a) only concerned with safeguarding individuals from interference with, or abuse by, the state and
b) focussed largely on the protection of defendants and prisoners?

---

21 *Doorson v Netherlands* [1996] 22 EHRR 330, para 70.

22 *X v UK*, [1992] 15 EHRR CD 113.

23 *Baegen v Netherlands* [1995] A/327-B, para 77.

24 Using similar reasoning, a rape trial was held to be not unfair even though the accused was not allowed to cross-examine a mentally unfit teenage victim in *HM Advocate v Nulty*, 2000 SCCR 431 (16 February 2000).

25 *McCourt v UK* [1993] 13 EHRR 379.

There are various layers to this but three stand out:

- Established principles of international law
- The evolution of human rights law and
- Our home grown tradition of civil liberties.

First, as is well known, no liability can be imposed on private individuals as a matter of international law. This means that all cases at the ECtHR must be taken against the government in question. This has led to the assumption that all such cases concern *state* violations *only*, when a growing number relate to abuses by private individuals or companies which states are obliged to protect other individuals from.

Second, there is a tendency to confuse first wave rights treaties from the Enlightenment era – like the French Declaration and American Bill of Rights which *were* preoccupied with freedom from *state* tyranny[26] – with the explosion of human rights treaties and declarations after the second world war, which had a broader focus.[27]

This second wave in rights evolution occurred partly in response to the calamitous events which preceded it. Individual responsibility for committing gross violations of human rights – in which 'just obeying orders' was not a legitimate excuse – was acknowledged by the Nuremburg trials for the first time.[28] Similarly, there was awareness that the scale of the Nazi atrocities could not have been accomplished without the active collaboration of thousands of individuals throughout Europe.

Just as important was the range of cultural and philosophical inputs into the Universal Declaration of Human Rights(UDHR) from which all subsequent UN human rights treaties flow. The influences on it[29] were far broader than the liberal, Western orientation of the French and American bills of rights. The delegates who drafted the UDHR were concerned to address the historic problem of how to protect individual rights without weakening the communities on which individuals depend. Values like dignity, equality and community underpin second wave rights charters as much as those of liberty and justice. The clearest manifestation of this orientation is found in

26 See F. Klug, *Values for a Godless Age, the story of the UK's new bill of rights* (Penguin, 2002), chapter 3.
27 ibid, chapter 4.
28 'International wrongs are committed by individuals and not by abstract entities', trial of the Major War Criminals, International Military Tribunal, Nuremberg 1946' 41 Am J Intl L 172.
29 These included Islam, Judaism, radical Christianity, Confucianism, Socialism, Social Democracy and Communism.

Article 29 of the UDHR, repeated in the preambles to the enforceable treaties which flowed from the Universal Declaration:[30]

> Everyone has duties to the community in which alone the free and full development of his [sic] personality is possible.

Limitations on rights, the Declaration continues, are therefore necessary to secure ' due recognition and respect for the rights and freedoms of others . . .'. This rationale for qualifying rights, flowing directly from the 'respect' individuals owe to the 'rights and freedoms of others', is contained in a modified form in the ECHR. The European Court of Human Rights continually emphasises that 'regard must be had to the fair balance that has to be struck between the competing interests of the individual and the community as a whole.'[31]

Third, the UK's indigenous human rights movement and allied lawyers have until recently worked in a legal environment in which there were no international human rights treaties incorporated into domestic law and we had no bill of rights or constitution. Since 2000 the ECHR has of course been part of our law and its broad provisions are imitative of a bill of rights.[32]

But much of the discourse around rights in the UK has not altered significantly from the pre-HRA era, when human rights bodies called themselves civil liberties organisations and human rights lawyers called themselves radical lawyers.

A literal, almost 'black-letter' approach to what is essentially a set of values expressed as broad legal principles is not uncommon. Every word in Article 6 of the ECHR, for example – the right to a fair trial – is exhaustively poured over for its possible meaning, by practitioners for whom some the open textured drafting of the ECHR is relatively new. Yet the ECtHR has continually emphasised that the crucial point is whether the proceedings *as a whole* are fair, rather than whether each individual sub-clause of Article 6 is technically observed in isolation, regardless of the consequence for competing values like public

---

30 The preambles to the twin instruments, the ICCPR and the ICESCR [adopted in 1966] state: 'Realising that the individual, having duties to other individuals and to the community to which he belongs, is under a responsibility to strive for the promotion and observance of the rights recognised in the present Covenant'.

31 eg *Powell and Rayner v UK* [1990] 12 EHRR 355. This approach has been explicitly adopted by UK judges applying the HRA, eg Lord Hope in *Clingham v Royal Borough of Kensington and Chelsea* [2002] UKHL 39 concerning classification of ASBOs as civil or criminal penalties.

32 Most notably section 2 which requires ECHR jurisprudence to be 'taken into account' but does not bind our courts to follow it, allowing other human rights treaties and jurisdictions' bills of rights to be cited.

safety[33]. This consideration can include an evaluation of the effects of Article 6 rights on other fundamental rights, as already explained.[34]

Through this route, a range of additional rights have effectively been 'read into' the right to a fair trial by the ECtHR including, as we gave have seen, protection of witnesses or victims but also other defendant's rights which are not directly referred to.[35] Consistent with this values-driven reasoning, 'only such measures restricting the rights of the defence which are *strictly* necessary are permissible under Article 6(1).'[36] [Emphasis added.]

The human rights approach to criminal justice

This paradigm provides the starting point for applying a human rights perspective to evaluating proposed reforms to the criminal justice system. It will only rarely produce clear-cut technical answers. More often it will provide a framework for assessing competing claims. The most contentious proposals in the current Criminal Justice Bill – concerning hearsay evidence, double jeopardy and 'bad character' evidence – illustrate this point.

Taking hearsay evidence first,[37] the Strasbourg court has developed three framework principles:

- evidence should be produced in a defendant's presence;
- the questioning of witnesses should be within an adversarial framework;
- defendants should be given an adequate and proper opportunity to challenge a witness at some stage during the proceedings.

However there are exceptions to this and reliance on hearsay evidence does not, in itself, necessarily breach the ECHR. Given the place accorded to the principle of justice in a democratic society, 'any measures restricting the rights of the defence should be strictly necessary;

---

33 *Rowe and Davies v UK* [2000] 30 EHRR 1, para 61. See also *Windisch v Austria* [1990] 13 EHRR 281; *Asch v Austria* [1991] 15 EHRR 597; *Ludi v Switzerland* [1992] 15 EHRR 173.

34 See note 21.

35 For example the right to participate effectively in criminal proceedings in *Stanford v UK* (1994). See also K. Starmer, *European Human Rights Law* (LAG, 1999), p260.

36 *Rowe and Davies v UK*, above, n33.

37 For the relevant provisions as enacted, see Criminal Justice Act 2003, Part 11, Chapter 2.

if a less restrictive measure can suffice that that measure should be applied.'[38] The question in each case is whether there has been overall fairness.[39] To be fair, convictions should not be based either solely or to a decisive extent on anonymous evidence.[40]

So in a case where the defendant was charged with unlawful sex with a young boy who was in intensive psychiatric care, the ECmHR determined that:

a) given that the interests of victims and witnesses are in principle protected by the ECHR;
b) the boy's psychiatrist gave live evidence instead, and
c) that there was other evidence to convict the accused,

the trial overall was fair.[41]

On the other hand, where an investigating judge in a Dutch case took witness statements from police officers but the defence did not know the identity of these witnesses who, during the trial, were protected from view by screens, this was judged to be a breach of ECHR Article 6.[42]

Moving on to double jeopardy, ECHR Protocol 7, Article 4, (which the UK has so far failed to ratify) restricts *retrials* for the same offence. However it explicitly exonerates 'the *re-opening* of [a] case in accordance with the law . . . if there is evidence of new or newly discovered facts or if there has been a fundamental defect in the previous proceedings which could effect the outcome of the case.'[43] The case law under Article 4 of Protocol 7 is almost entirely devoted to double punishment for the same offence rather than retrials.

The equivalent provision in the ICCPR (Article 14(7)) appears not to have the same 'get out 'for re-opening trials as the ECHR. But the 'General Comment' of the UN's Human Rights Committee – which seeks to clarify the scope of this clause – implies endorsement of the practice of 'most states' which 'make a clear distinction between a resumption of a trial *justified by exceptional circumstances* and a re-trial prohibited by the principle of ne bis in idem.'[44] [emphasis added.]

38 *Van Mechelen and others v Netherlands*, [1997] 25 EHRR 647, para 59.
39 *Unterpertinger v Austria* [1986] 13 EHRR 175. See also note 23.
40 *Doorson v Netherlands*, above, n21.
41 *MK v Austria*, [1997] 24 EHRR CD 59.
42 *Van Mechelen and others v Netherlands*, above n38.
43 Clause 2. Clause 1 reads: 'No one shall be liable to be tried or punished again in criminal proceedings under the jurisdiction of the same state for an offence for which he has already been finally acquitted or convicted in accordance with the law on penal procedure of that State'.
44 *General Comment No.13* (13.04.84) UN Human Rights Committee.

The UK's Joint Committee on Human Rights found the government's original proposals to order a second trial (a)only at the behest of the Court of Appeal[45] and (b) only where *compelling* evidence was found which ' was not available or known to an officer or prosecutor at the time of the acquittal' broadly compatible with international human rights law.[46]

Under the government's amended proposals – which the Joint Committee does not support – 'new evidence' has been defined to mean that which 'was not adduced in the proceedings in which the person was acquitted.'[47] This arguably permits a new hearing on the grounds of evidence that could have been, but was not, used at the earlier trial and on the face of it could let sloppy original investigations off the hook.

On the other hand, the more that the new permissible evidence is restricted to what is classified as *compelling* new evidence, the more difficult it is to argue – using the ECtHR benchmark of the 'fairness of the proceedings as a whole' – that a defendant will receive a 'fair trial' in which the presumption of innocence prevails.

The UN Human Rights' Committee's 'General Comment' refers to a resumption of trials 'justified by exceptional *circumstances*'[48] – which is not the same as exceptional or compelling *evidence*. This might be deemed to refer to situations like multiple murderers or rapes, for example, where new evidence comes to light, compelling or otherwise, that links a previously acquitted defendant with the crime. The exceptional circumstance could be the clear and present risk to the right to life of others that would prevail should the suspect be free to strike again. As we have seen, the state is duty-bound to take preventative action to protect fundamental rights.[49]

Turning finally to so-called bad character evidence, the ECtHR has repeatedly said that neither the 'presumption of innocence' enshrined in Article 6(2), nor the 'equality of arms' provision in adversarial circumstances contained in Article 6(3), require states to adopt

---

45 Which, arguably, conforms with the description 're-opening of a case' – permitted under the ECHR and ICCPR – rather than 're-trial' at the behest of the prosecutor, which may not.

46 Joint Committee on Human Rights, Second Report, Session 2002–3, Criminal Justice Bill, HL Paper 40, HC 374, paras 43–52.

47 Joint Committee on Human Rights, *Criminal Justice Bill: Further Report* (Eleventh report of Session 2002–3), para 36. See Criminal Justice Act 2003 s78.

48 See n44.

49 See n17.

specific rules concerning admissibility of evidence. These are matters principally for regulation under domestic law.[50]

The ECtHR has not established any specific rule about the permissibility of bad character evidence and the Law Commission tells us that in a number of states which are signatories to the ECHR lists of previous convictions are routinely presented by the prosecution.[51] As is well known, 'similar fact evidence' and evidence of the lack of the defendant's credibility as a witness are already permitted.

The human rights question, therefore, is the precise terms of the extension of 'bad character evidence' and its effect on the fairness of the trial as a whole. It is difficult, in particular, to see how it is fair, overall, to include evidence that 'the person has behaved, or is disposed to behave, in a way that, in the opinion of the court, might be viewed with disapproval by a reasonable person.'[52] It is difficult to entirely remove the suspicion that this provision is rather more about increasing clear up rates – by indirectly encouraging the police to roundup the 'usual suspects' and so-called 'undesirables' – than increasing the protection of individuals from violent crime.

It is equally hard to understand how a 'disapproval' provision is *necessary* and *proportionate* to protect the fundamental rights of vulnerable individuals. If it was convincingly demonstrated that the provision was absolutely necessary to save lives and protect other fundamental rights, and the discretion given to the judge to control the use of such evidence meant the proceedings were still fair *overall*, the conclusion, in human rights terms, might be different. The Law Commission, in their recent report on the non-accidental death of children, refreshingly acknowledge that ' to focus' almost exclusively on Article 6 rights – as they had originally done in considering how to reform the law – 'was an unbalanced approach'. It 'failed to give sufficient weight to other, *even more fundamental* human rights which are in play' such as the right to life or freedom from inhumane treatment of children.[53] [Emphasis added.]

---

50   *Schenk v Switzerland* [1991] 13 EHRR 242; *Barbera, Messegué and Jabardo v Spain* (1988) Application No 00010590/83.

51   *Evidence of Bad Character in Criminal Proceedings*, Law Commission, No 273, 2001.

52   The definition of bad character in clause 81 of the Bill was amended and now refers to 'evidence of, or of a disposition towards, misconduct on [the defendant's] part'. See Criminal Justice Act 2003 s98.

53   Law Commission Report, *Children: their non-accidental death or serious injury (criminal trials)*, No. 279, 2003, paras 4.8 & 4.16.

Conclusion

Victims, as we have seen, are (or should be) central to human rights thinking. This is not to suggest that 'the victim' is viewed in the same way in human rights law as in domestic criminal law. Nor are victims conceived of as an 'interest group' in the sense that some victims groups might represent them.

Human rights law is based on a set of values that seeks to root out abuse of power – from whichever source – and secure respect for the essential dignity of every individual. As such, the framework in which victims' human rights has evolved gives a distinctive emphasis to psychological harm, privacy, the effective investigation of crimes, protection from intimidation in court, and even the effect on 'indirect victims' like close family members,[54] as well as the obligation on the state to prosecute suspects and deter crimes.

The state has a special role in international human rights law as the body charged with remedying abuses, whether by refraining from acting oppressively itself or preventing and restraining private parties from doing so. Whilst the origins of human rights law began with a focus on state violations, the search for remedies of abuse of power inexorably led it to embrace private power as well.

It was feminist literature and the women's movement which provided the original critique of a public law model of human rights which failed to recognise that for one gender, abuse within the home could be as much, if not more, oppressive than abuse by the state.[55] More recently anti-racist, children's and anti-capitalist critiques of human rights have developed this argument further.

The focus on defendants' and prisoners rights by human rights defenders – as crucial as these obviously are – can give the impression that the only victims human rights law is *really* concerned to protect are offenders and that the *true* abusers are the offenders' real-life victims who wish to limit their rights. In this Alice in Wonderland world it is not difficult for the Home Secretary to play the part of the Queen of Hearts and shout 'off with their heads' every time he spots a lawyer or judge. The sleepy dormouse – sadly – can be human rights.

---

54 eg *Kurt v Turkey*, 25/5/98, Application No 00024276/94, 27 EHRR 373.
55 See for example C. MacKinnon, *Feminism Unmodified: Discourses on Life and Law* (Harvard University Press, 1987) pp3 and 104, and *Towards a Feminist Theory of the State* (Harvard University Press, 1989) pp187–90; K. O'Donovan, *Sexual Divisions in Law* (Weidenfeld & Nicholson, 1985) pp7–8.

If we are to move on from this Mad Hatter's tea party then we need greater clarity about the role of victims in human rights thinking. To this end, we need a consistent appreciation of both the founding values and evolutionary nature of international human rights law, As former UN Special Rapporteur on minorities, Erica Irene-Daes, once memorably remarked:

> The world community should accept the thesis that the seat of human rights is primarily in the conscience of mankind and then in moral and positive law.

CHAPTER 10

Balancing the rights of victims and offenders

By Barbara Hudson
Professor of Law, University of Central Lancashire

Introduction

I was pleased to be invited to contribute to this seminar series on victims' rights and the rightful role of victims in the criminal justice system. The difficulty with taking part in the final seminar is the fear that everything that could be said has already been said. In this case, certainly a great deal has been said in previous seminars, and there is much of great value in the previous papers, much that I would wish to endorse. Views that I would wish particularly to support from earlier seminars are:

- that it is beyond question that victims have rights to respect and to be kept informed of the process of trials
- that victims should be well supported and adequately compensated
- that defendants' due process rights must be maintained and protected
- that some recent developments and proposals threaten to undermine fairness to defendants

The principle I want to emphasise is encapsulated in the title of this paper: that the question of victims' and defendants' rights is a question of balance. Both groups have rights and neither sets of rights should be sacrificed. This balance is extremely difficult, so much so that it is probably impossible to achieve a perfectly just equilibrium. Criminal justice systems here and elsewhere demonstrate pendulum shifts between favouring defence and prosecution, victims' rights and offenders' rights. The balance is almost inevitably slightly wrong; what matters is to maintain the sense of balance, rather than the zero 125 sum political mentality that seems to have been around lately, that what is good for victims must be bad for offenders. The political/popular idea that offenders have too many rights needs to be challenged at the same time that the idea that victims may have too few rights needs to be supported.

In this paper I first raise some questions about the status of 'victim'. I then argue for more 'discursiveness' in criminal justice, and then go on to think about two problematic categories of persons for considerations of balance in criminal justice: the potential victim, and the offender for whom it is difficult to have sympathy. I conclude by revisiting the question of balance and the importance of its maintenance.

Who is a victim?

'Victim' is not an unproblematic category in criminal justice. Which victim is it who should have more rights; which rights should attach to which kinds of victims? It is not true to say that victims are excluded from criminal justice. Victims are at the very heart of criminal justice; it is because some harm has been perpetrated against a victim that criminal justice processes are set into play. What is the case, and what is the real meaning of the objection that victims have until now been excluded from criminal justice, is that the victim's role is assumed by the state. The state-as-victim construction is what differentiates criminal law from civil law; it is what distinguishes crime from tort, crime is a wrong against the state and its moral rules, as well as a harm done to another individual. This assumption of the victim role by the state in criminal law is obviously a truism and something that 'everybody knows', but its implications are significant for the question of balancing rights.

The power imbalance between the state and the individual defendant is what makes due process safeguards for defendants so necessary, and is why they must vigilantly be maintained. Until the current punitive, vengeful turn of penal politics, the main calls for victims' rights in criminal justice processes concerned the relationship between individual, actual victims and the state-as-victim, rather than the relationship between individual victims and offenders. Some critics saw the state as 'usurping' the role of victims, as 'stealing' harms away from victims and offenders, and advocated criminal justice models more akin to civil justice.[1]

1   N. Christie, 'Conflicts as property', Br J Criminol, 1977 17: 1–15.

Even if formal criminal justice with its state-as-victim construct is defended, it is now more generally acknowledged that the restricted role of prosecution witness that this leaves for actual victims, is unsatisfactory. They need to be able to tell their harm directly and fully, and they need to be given support, protection and actual information. As well as victim support, witness protection, victim information and victim compensation schemes, one response to the marginalisation of individual victims in criminal justice proceedings has been the development of restorative justice, which allows victims and offenders to tell their own stories, in their own words, and with support from family and others. I certainly welcome the inclusion of restorative justice in the repertoire of responses to crime, but I have also urged greater discursive openness in traditional, formal criminal justice processes.[2]

Victims, it is generally agreed, should not only be able to tell their stories, they also have claims to recompense and to support services.[3] What is more controversial is the role that victims' suffering and victims' accounts should play in sentencing. Again, the crux of the issue is the differentiation between state-as-victim and the individual victim; between a standard victim and a particular victim. Law necessarily operates with categories of harms and wrongs that generalise victims and their sufferings. This may seem to do less than justice to the individual, actual victim. Some efforts have been made to clarify understandings of degrees of harm, such as Von Hirsch and Jareborg's 'living standards' classification, where degrees of harm correspond to the impact on the victim's quality of life.[4] The Criminal Justice Act 1991 recognised the fact that different sorts of victims might be more or less harmed (their quality of life might be more or less damaged) by the same sort of crime. Targeting – demonstrated by repeat offences – of particular groups such as the elderly, people with whom the offender had a relationship of trust, minority ethnic citizens, being considered aggravating factors seems a practical and reasonable way of recognising the differences in the amount of suffering caused by 'the same' kind of crime.

2   B. Hudson, 'Victims and Offenders' in A. von Hirsch, J. Roberts, A. Bottoms, K. Roach and M. Schiff (eds), *Restorative Justice and Criminal Justice: Competing or Reconcilable Paradigms* (Hart, 2002).
3   These topics are well covered by earlier papers in this volume, so they do not need discussion here.
4   A. von Hirsch and N. Jareborg, 'Gauging harm to others: a living standard analysis' in A. von Hirsch and A. Ashworth (eds), *Principled Sentencing* (Edinburgh University Press, 1992).

Going beyond this to a much more individualised calculus of harm, for example by allowing victim impact statements to influence sentencing, does, however, cause concerns from the point of view of fairness to offenders. For example, for opportunist rather than carefully targeted burglaries, it would surely be unfair if burglars of apparently similar premises, committed whilst the occupant was out, were punished differently if one victim was a laid-back individual, well insured and quite able to take the burglary in her stride, while another was someone who was severely traumatised.

These difficulties can arise with restorative justice as well as with formal criminal justice. John Braithwaite, one of the leading advocates of restorative justice, has considered the possibility of an unusually vengeful victim or an unusually sensitive victim claiming more than ordinary harm and so demanding out-of-the-ordinary levels of recompense or punitive impositions, or refusing to accept restorative processes and outcomes where other victims of 'the same' offence would agree.[5] Braithwaite also mentions the possibility of a dishonest victim, claiming more loss than has actually been suffered. These concerns about the influence individual victims should have on measures imposed by restorative justice proceedings have led some advocates to re-evaluate the importance of proportionality, and to introduce proportionality as a standard for restorative justice.

Another complication in giving actual, individual victims a larger role in criminal justice is that who is a victim is not an unproblematic issue, and, moreover, the distinction between victims and offenders is not as clear-cut as some of the arguments about victims' rights make it appear. There is a *hierarchy of credibility* associated with victimhood.[6] Some kinds of people are more credible as victims than others. Rather than being a dichotomy victim/offender, there is a continuum between the two statuses. At one end of the continuum, black men have the least credibility as victims, at the other, white women have the most. White men and black women are between the two ends of the continuum.

This is illustrated by the Stephen Lawrence case, and other high-profile cases involving black victims. Stephen Lawrence was first of all seen as part of the trouble, someone who would be participating in a

---

5   J. Braithwaite, 'Restorative justice: assessing optimistic and pessimistic accounts', in M. Tonry (ed), *Crime and Justice: A Review of Research, vol 25,* (University of Chicago Press, 1999).

6   N. Christie, 'The Ideal Victim' in E. Fatah (ed), *From Crime Policy to Victim Policy* (Macmillan, 1986).

fight, not as the innocent victim he is now known to be. It is also well-established that white, middle-class, 'respectable' women have greater success than other kinds of women in claiming the status of rape victim and being believed when they insist they did not consent to intercourse. Research also demonstrates that white women offenders with a persuasive solicitor and/or probation officer are frequently constructed as victims – of abusive or coercive males, of poverty, of addictions – and so not as fully to blame for their crimes.[7] Sentencing research, especially in the USA, demonstrates variations in sentencing according to the racial characteristics of victims as well as of offenders.[8]

My own research looks at some of the processes which lead to differential sentencing, and shows that black offenders are held more to blame for factors such as unemployment than white offenders are; with white offenders, their unemployment is seen as a pressure leading to crime so that their unemployment explains their crime; with black offenders their criminality is seen as making them unable to get or keep a job, so that their crime explains their unemployment. A study I have recently completed in north west England shows that young Asian men involved in assaults on white offenders do not have their claims to racial provocation taken seriously; such claims are categorised as 'refusal to accept responsibility' and so make them more liable to custodial sentences.[9]

Allowing individual victims to influence sentencing, therefore, might lead to unanticipated consequences. Not only might sentencing reflect disparities in the amount of suffering related by victims, and the extent to which offenders are seen as totally to blame or partly as victims themselves, but sentences and levels of support and compensation might also reflect differences in credibility and sympathy extended differentially on account of personal or social characteristics of victims themselves.

Actual individual victims, then, ought to have access to support services, to state funded compensation, to information and to protection; they should be treated with respect and they should be able to relate their experiences in their own words, without having to confine

7   K. Daly, *Gender, Crime and Punishment* (Yale University Press, 1994).

8   G. Kleck, 'Racial Discrimination in Criminal Sentencing: A Critical Evaluation of the Evidence with Additional Evidence on the Death Penalty', *American Sociological Review* 1981 46: 783–805.

9   G. Bramhall and B. Hudson, *Criminal Justice and Racial Equality: A Report for Lancashire Probation Service* (unpublished report, 2002).

themselves to replies to questions. But differences in the sensibilities of victims to harms inflicted, and differences in their emotional responses to 'their' offenders, as well as differences in the importance and credibility given to victims' experiences and to offenders circumstances, lead me to be wary of extending of victims' rights to include influencing sentencing.

Risk of re-offending

The figure who has become more dominant in penal policy in the late 1990s and into the 2000s is not the actual victim, but the *potential* victim. Risk of re-offending has become an *over*-emphasised concern in recent policy developments. I say over-emphasised, because risk of re-offending clearly is a legitimate and central concern of criminal justice; but the importance it is presently given may be such as to conflict with justice for offenders.

There is always tension between crime control aims and due process values such as fairness and consistency. In penal theory, these different aspects of criminal justice are usually termed utilitarian and retributive functions of punishment, the former oriented towards crime control and the latter towards dispensing a just measure of deserved punishment. The one is forward-looking (towards crimes yet to be – possibly – committed); the other is backward-looking (towards crimes actually and already committed). For penal philosophers, the question of principle is whether or not it is ever justifiable to penalise people for acts they may do in the future. For policymakers and criminal justice professionals, the question is how the balance is to be struck between crime control and justice.

There are several suggested compromises between utilitarian targets and retributive constraints.[10] One of the most influential is *limiting retributivism*, an approach largely associated with Norval Morris and Michael Tonry. Morris's notion of limiting retributivism is that proportionality should set the outer limits to the punishment that may be imposed for any offence; crime control concerns should be pursued within those limits.[11] Tonry modifies the theory by arguing that *parsimony* is a more important principle than proportionality in limiting

10 B. Hudson, *Understanding Justice* (Open University Press, 2nd ed, 2003), chapter 4.

11 N. Morris, 'Desert as a limiting principle', in A. von Hirsch and A. Ashworth (eds), *Principled Sentencing* (Edinburgh University Press, 1992).

retributivism.[12] Parsimony dictates that proportionality should set only the upper limits to punishment; the actual punishment should be the least restrictive penalty with the possibility of achieving crime reduction objectives. This is a very different approach to punishment than the mandatory minimum, three-strikes, 'flat-line' penalties that are becoming a more pronounced part of UK as well as US penal systems, and at first glance it perhaps seems balanced too far in favour of offenders and too far against potential victims.

In a critique of the Halliday Report,[13] Tonry and Rex say that limiting retributivism is one of the key principles of the new proposals.[14] They argue, however, that the principle of proportionality as setter of limits is only weakly incoporated, and that parsimony is even more weakly adhered to than proportionality is. Although Halliday recommends a sentencing council to promulgate presumptive sentencing bands for each offence category (thereby establishing proportionality), risk of re-offending will influence whether an offender receives a custody, custody-plus or custody-minus sentence. The powers and stringent expectations of recall to prison for any breaches of supervision conditions mean that risk of re-offending can significantly influence the amount of the term served in custody, because the greater the risk of re-offending, the more restrictive and demanding will be the conditions of supervision, and therefore the higher the likelihood of breach.

What is so disturbing about the place of risk of re-offending in these proposals is that the sentences in question are *short* custodial sentences, sentences of less than 12 months. Some of the terms envisaged range from two weeks to three months. These are people whose offences are not so serious, nor whose presence on the streets is so dangerous to potential victims, that they need to be incarcerated for public protection for very long periods. This use of risk assessment in short sentences marks a radical departure from the philosophy of the Criminal Justice Act 1991. In that Act, sentencing could be more-than-proportionate because of risk in the case of serious violent and sexual offences, but for other offences proportionality was to determine sentences. Rehabilitation, reform, and other crime control goals could be incorporated into work done with the offender during

---

12 M. Tonry, 'Proportionality, Parsimony and Interchangeability of Punishments', in A. Duff and D. Garland (eds), *A Reader on Punishment* (OUP, 1994).

13 J. Halliday, *Making Punishments Work: Review of the Sentencing Framework for England and Wales* (Home Office, 2001).

14 M. Tonry and S. Rex, *Reform and Punishment: The future of sentencing* (Willan, 2002).

terms either in prison or in the community, but proportionality to current offence was to determine sentence length and severity.

Shifting offences that warrant short sentences (and where there is discretion to give non-custodial sentences) from the proportionality to the risk track demonstrates a diminution of the importance of the difference between violent and non violent crimes. At the beginning of the 1990s, there was shared understanding that departures from proportionality because of risk were justified only if the harm risked was of serious violence – in other words, if the offender was dangerous. Less serious offences, even if persistent, were not to alter the balance between offenders' rights and potential victims' rights. Although there was some blurring of the divide because of the inclusion of 'psychological harm' (which could be trauma resulting from burglary, for example), nonetheless there was general agreement – at least among penal professionals – that persistence of itself did not justify more-than-proportionate punishment. As the 1990s progressed, and continuing into the 2000s, dangerousness and persistence were increasingly bracketed together.[15]

Proposals in the Halliday Report, and legislation stemming from it, suggest that risk assessment can make a very significant difference to sentencing of offenders convicted of less serious property offences, whether risk is indicated by previous convictions, or by factorial risk assessment when release on licence is being considered. In the first case, the result could be more severe penalties because of record; in the second case, the result could be more of the sentence spent in custody rather than in the community. In either case, the balance between offenders' rights and potential victims' rights is changed. The balance should be such that extended sentencing (as provided for in the criminal justice bill currently before Parliament)[16] or enhanced sentencing should only be available where the risk to potential victims is serious physical harm; where this sort of danger is not present, then the offenders' obligations to society should be met through sentencing proportionate to the seriousness of the current offence.

The traditional balance between offenders' rights and potential victims' rights used to reflect *risk management*; the new balance reflects *risk control*.[17] Risk management means that the criminal

---

15 See for example, the White Paper, *Protecting the Public* (Home Office, 1996).

16 Criminal Justice Act 2003 ss227 and 228.

17 T. Clear and E. Cadora, 'Risk and Community Practice' in K. Stenson and R. R. Sullivan (eds), *Crime, Risk and Justice: The politics of crime control in liberal democracies* (Willan, 2001).

justice system will attempt to improve the management of risk by better rehabilitative and treatment programmes, better risk assessment, more support for offenders in the community, while accepting the inevitability of some degree of failure: some offenders will re-offend. Risk management means accepting responsibilities to reduce crime as much as reasonably possible without denying offenders' rights to proportionate treatment and to enjoyment of reasonable liberty on release, and the goal is a fair balance between public protection and offenders' rights. Risk control means intolerance of any degree of risk, seeking to exclude the risky person from social participation, whether through incarceration, curfews and restrictions, or, of course, in some jurisdictions, through execution. Risk control aims toward the elimination of risk, an unachievable aim which therefore provokes more and more punitive demands. Present policies are taking us too far in the direction of risk control.

The monstrous offender

The other criminal justice character who raises questions about the balance of rights between victims and offenders is the offender with whom it is difficult to sympathise. Criminal justice is best suited to dealing with offenders who commit (statistically and psychologically) normal crimes; offenders whose motivations can be understood, even while their acts are disapproved and their reasoning found wanting. Most of us might disapprove of stealing and other forms of dishonesty, but we can at least understand the young man for whom burglary seems the only available career option, or the young mother whose child will be made fun of if he doesn't have the fashionable kind of trainers, and so she accepts knocked off goods at knock down prices. The moral distance between these 'ordinary' offenders and ourselves is not too great: how many of us check the provenance of items at car boot sales or antique fairs? But there are some offenders with whom it is impossible to sympathise, whether the repulsion felt towards them derives from their actions or from their personalities.

Criminal justice depends to a large extent on understanding to ensure the balance between offenders and victims. If we cannot understand why someone did something, we cannot see what might discourage them from doing it again; the instinct towards vengeance and exclusion steps in to fill the void of understanding.

Discursive justice, whether by this we mean restorative justice, or allowing more opportunities for victims and offenders to tell their stories within formal court proceedings, can only be effective if some understanding can be achieved. The victim will not feel reassured – no restoration can take place – unless she can understand why the offender committed the crime; the offender cannot offer restoration, cannot undertake rehabilitative work, unless he can understand the harm caused. Doubts about the use of restorative justice in sexualised violence cases, whether within a domestic setting or not, often centre on whether there can be understanding if there are two radically differing perspectives, hers and his. If there is no reciprocity of perspectives – no sense that if I were in her shoes, I might act in the same way – then there can be no understanding, no sympathy, no restoration.

Discursive justice, then, has limits of comprehensibility, as does formal justice. To do justice to someone involves recognising their selfhood, their circumstances and motivations, their hopes and fears – this applies to victims and to offenders. If someone is convicted of something we cannot imagine ourselves doing in any conceivable circumstances, then we have difficulty in seeing them as a fellow citizen, and then it is easy and tempting to move towards responding to them as something other than human, as monsters. There is a worrying tendency to use dehumanising language to describe more and more offenders. Sexual predators are described as 'animals', but so are more ordinary criminals. Remember the television crime prevention campaign that portrayed car thieves as jackals? Remember too the young offender known as 'rat boy' in Newcastle? The nickname came from his habit of evading arrest by going through the central heating pipes of his estate: this implies that he was small, but people attending court when he was finally convicted said they were surprised how small he was; they had been expecting a giant rat, a monster.

What seems to be happening is that rare and grave crimes – the killing of James Bulger and Sarah Payne, terrorists who kill civilians, for example – lead to augmentation of punitiveness and vengefulness, and exceptional cases become templates for dealing with more normal cases; horror and revulsion become generalised from exceptional criminals to general classes of criminals. If we cannot understand and we cannot sympathise, the only framework we have to ensure that we do not cross the bounds of humane dealing, is rights. In this era of insecurity, lack of solidarity, risk consciousness and apprehension of danger as described by the risk society theorists, it is more important than ever that we maintain strong adherence to the idea of inalienable human rights, amongst which are the rights of fair trial and the right not to be punished other than for an offence of which one has been fairly convicted.[18] We must resist the fashionable communitarian idea that rights must be earned, and can be forfeited if persons do not behave responsibly. Some lesser rights may be forfeited, but these should only be lower level civil rights, not the core of fundamental human rights.[19]

Conclusions: real offenders and actual victims

Criminal justice seems to be becoming dominated by the images of the monstrous offender and the ideological victim. Offenders are being dehumanised and treated as anything but fellow-citizens. Victims – especially potential victims – are being invoked ideologically as justification for eroding the rights of offenders. Real, flesh-and-blood victims need support, protection, the right to tell their story in their own way, and they need to be reassured that steps will be taken to prevent their future victimisation, by this or any other offender. But offenders are also humans, and have rights to proportionate punishment, to punishment which is commensurate with what they have done, not what they might do in the future.

If rights are to be balanced, rather than the rights of one group sacrificed to those of the other, then the principle that all should enjoy life, freedom from violation, and as much freedom as is consistent with the like rights of others, must apply. This entails not more-than-proportionate exclusion from society because of predictions that an offender might commit a further offence (a prediction which cannot be disproved if the offender is incarcerated), but the provision of robust support in the community to help offenders refrain from crime, and obligations on offenders to participate in programmes designed to prevent future offending. Upholding victims' rights also means that states should be held accountable for provision or failure to provide suitable projects and supports.

Programmes such as the befriending circles that have been successfully developed in Canada to provide support for sex offenders in the community are the sort of scheme that balances rights of victims to protection from further crime with offenders' rights to participate in society once they have served the commensurate penalty, and are

18 B. Hudson, *Justice in the Risk Society* (Sage, 2003).
19 A. Ashworth, *Human Rights, Serious Crime and Criminal Procedure*, The Hamlyn Lectures (Sweet and Maxwell, 2002)

to be preferred to schemes which restrict ex-offenders' rights and liberties once they have served their penalty.

Victims clearly have rights; potential victims are owed crime prevention programmes short of curtailing of fundamental rights of (ex-)offenders. As Dworkin puts it, (potential) victims' rights to safety might well be more important than offenders' rights to liberty; but if they are both *rights* then they are both the same category of thing, so that the one cannot be everything and the other nothing.[20]

20 R. Dworkin, *Taking Rights Seriously* (Harvard University Press, 1978).